Please note that this work features
provocative
dancing

ANIMAL NOISES: LYRICS ETC. 2001-2022

Published by Continuous Breath

www.dizraeli.com

The right of Rowan Sawday to be identified as the author of this work has been asserted by him in accordance with Section 77 of the Copyright, designs and Patent Act 1988.

Illustrations: Dizraeli
Book design: Amy Acre
Turntables: Dj DownLow
Self-loathing: Timothy
Trumpets: Leroy Merlin
Outside eye: Anthony Anaxagorou

ISBN: 978-1-913268-37-4

Printed in the UK by Print Resources


by the time you wake
by crook, hook and middle eight
by twist of phrase
by the spin on things
by the fierce green hearts of trees
by the gangbangs of spring
and the scream that empties everything
by the dying engine
by the crushed cicada
by the one black ant left standing
holding the last solitary black seed
then the up-rising of the whole
gurt stinking parade
again and again and again

7/7/22. Ashton Court

The place is what comes through. The song is always from a place. The mountain-tree, the mother with her orange son, making making making. This beautiful dead place, these pretty corpses, brilliant from a million corners in details no human could falsify. All of it writing, working, making a book. The book gives its fire, the woman sits with her eyes closed, the dog bickers with an unseen mole, a thistle sways drunkly, the man in green at the glass table writes what he sees, making

a book of my song lyrics, from early to most recent, and I want it to give out the warmth that I feel and also to fling windows open, so anyone can see inside, see the mess a song rises from, slithers sideways out of, stays writhing in.

The song by itself is a hologram; the actual flesh of it is the mess of Bristol, Green Lanes, Ashton Court; the human bodies sweating, uncertain. Dirty.

god chuckles.

Part of me still wants to pretend, to use this book to project something (edgy writelord of the edgeworld scuffing through the far alleys, in the shadows where the dangers are etc, bringing reports back from the unterland etc) but a bigger part of me sees that and smiles: none of me can know what'll be received and by who, and Jesus these are the End Times who gives a fuck who's edgy. Edge off, edgelord, leave space for the actual flesh, the gubbins and broken toes, the promises that we are hanged from, love that doesn't look like love, the whole fruit-palace of unrepeatable splendour that rises everywhere in every instant.

This book then. It is made of songs that are already out there and in the earholes, the cars and living rooms and private darks of humans, songs brought together here to make a book that spreads her hands honestly and says, "here's what really happened"

or maybe

"Here's what this man-boy wanted people to see him as, in the autumn of 2010. 2007, 2002."

Some of these songs I see now are crammed with armour, self-protections, half lies. Some of them are cringemaking to me now, bad or preachy or dated. But they all somehow found people to resonate in. They've bounced around the human world making their noises, causing people's chemicals to surge or subside in ways that have helped, I am told. So I stand them here as they were made, often alongside the doodled creatures that accompanied their births, and some tangential scribblings and stinky rhymeschemes that composted into better ideas.

The beetle is the forest as much as the trees. There are beetles here, as well as worms from the substrata that galvanise arboreousness from the blah blah shut up.

Ah, Timothy.

Alright then miraculous One, here it is :

Animal Noises.

# ANIMAL NOISES

Lyrics etc
2001 - 2022

# DIZRAELI

# Contents

# EARLY DAYS
2001-2009

# Bad Science

*Bad Science existed from 1999-2008. It was born as a hiphop & drum n bass night in Bristol which moved to Brighton and became a band : me, Jer, Alex, Tom and sometimes J-top, Sam and Mason.*

*Here is me at that time : I want to save the world from the madness of capitalism / I want everyone to get naked / I want to be Jim Morrison.*

*This is a handful of lyrics from those songs. Part of me wants to strike them from the record : they aren't good enough. But they are where I started, and as such, here they are.*

## THE ESSENCE (2001)

The day rises / spreading warm over the shape of the countryside
I greet the sun as the ocean below greets the tide
Perched here on the edge of an abstract landscape
Shadows draped under dew-soaked trees / I unsedate
Wakened / but taking my time still
The chill of the dawn fades / I'm feeling a quiet thrill
A thrill in the ease and slowness of holidays
I stretch myself on grass and inhale the haze
of the pollen-heavy sweet-scented air I lie under
I allow myself to drift, and my thoughts wander
Taking in the pure release of head unstoppered
with the innocent sensuality of a child stuffing chocolate
into open mouth I cram in ideas unrestrained
Again and again / a rush of knowledge embraces brain
I am what I be / label me at own risk

You can't hack passion, beauty or the fact I'm a pacifist
I will not be beaten down or dismissed
and I will not wear the confines of time on my wrist
and the abyss between us and the essence widens
Grown men push pens and pretend to be titans
Well I'm a giant / sat in my field introspecting
marvelling at the view / and my own imperfection
I begin to write / to exercise my own blessings
and as the ink traces out these words
it's the essence

When lyrics drip from betwixt lips
it's the essence
When sun sets and drums get hit
it's the essence
When people sing sick of the shit
it's the essence
Dance naked with a weightless spirit
Taste the essence

The day has moved on / the sun squats fat upon horizon
The sea is given over / to the whims of Poseidon
Still I'm stuck to this raised ground / I sit to create
Panoramic eyes let me see the many parts relate.
Up here the air's clear / trees root, reach and grow
You can almost imagine that you can't hear the road
cutting scars in the hillside
Never mind / as long as the weather's kind
My conscience is better blind
Sometimes I cease forever trying to preach
Leave the global / just inhabit what my senses reach

and this field is just that / as the dusk tumbles down
a bonfire is blazed / friends and darkness gather round
Skins are paired / tales and rhymes are shared
Woodsmoke billows and clings to clothes and hair
and we become one another in strange ways
Harmonised lives as a battered guitar plays
familiar tunes / and constellations bloom in the blackness
as though given life by our breath
and there's no trace of doubt in my restful head
and there's no hint of malice in any words said
Steadily the heady rhythm swells / some chant and some dance
Having abandoned inhibition / we whirl in a trance
You may laugh at this hippy / or feel threatened
but I've known freedom
and it's the essence...

When lyrics drip from betwixt lips
it's the essence
When sun sets and drums get hit
it's the essence
When people sing sick of the shit
it's the essence
Dance naked with a weightless spirit
Taste the essence

# MR POLITICIAN (2004)

Mr Politician on the television
What's happening behind those eyes?
While your serpent tongue goes on with its clever twisting
And your collar is uncomfortably tight...
Mr Politician, do you believe you?
Because I feel as though I've heard this talk before
Do you laugh, do you giggle, do you bleed too?
Does your body have a human sort of warm?

Mr Politician on the television
You've lost me, man
Can you speak English please?
Although yours is an interesting kind of fiction
There are some real answers that we need...

And to my surprise

He replied...
*Substantial increases in threats from criminal forces have led us to conclude
that a conclusion should be reached and this report suggests that measures
should be taken as regards the situation of interracial relations and ancillary
organisational effectiveness as clearly stated in section six of the ninth chapter
of the recent enquiry at no point did we deceive the people it was merely a
question of finding the weapons which we knew were there with absolute
probable certainty, probably and what matters is that this is Duh...*

*what matters is that this is Duh...*
*What matters is that this is*
*Democracy!*
*And they're better off now than ever before!*
*This is a just war*
*This is a just war*
*This is just a war....*

Mr Politician on the television
What's the purpose of your oratory games
What are you thinking while you're sitting shitting?
Do you call your wife by an affectionate name?
And when's the last time you cried, Mr Politician?
Do you sleep well at night, Mr Politician?
Come and stand by my side, Mr Politician
And taste a little bit of life before you die.

## MOTHS (2007)

I trace a path across the madness of the nightlife
Seeing the clubbers come like moths to the bright lights
They'll flutter in the heat for a while before they fall
Spiralling in a world of sweat and mirror balls
Spirits trawling for a chance to let go of it all
Staggering beneath the streetlamps and pissing on walls
Staggering beneath the streetlamps and pissing on walls

and we fall / one by one...

I can't help but giggle / feeling in my pockets for change
to buy enough drugs to let me get a taste of the deranged
Then I'm away / back at the flat / a cold beer to warm my mind
It's me and my friends / chatting bollocks, taking our time
A cheeky line to fuel another pint / to fuel us heading for the outside
where drizzle falls and sirens cry
Fuck it though, we're on a roll and we're in the flow of things
Isn't a minute goes by without a phone rings
Plans are made / and we're off to the spot where tonight's crew are gathering
We laugh and catch up on the happenings
Scrabbling for the bar / Ai Tequila for my first round
I drop a half a bean to let my body feel the sound
Steady caress / ready to rush 'til the dawn of day
Just give me chemistry and I can... oh
Steady caress / ready to rush 'til the dawn of day
Just give me chemistry and I can fly away...

Cos the beer is for the friendship / whisky's for the winter freeze
Poppers are for the comeup / wallet's for the entry fees
Ecstasy's for the love, passion and depression
Viagra is for fucking / vodka's for forgetting
The cocaine is for the self-esteem
The acid's for the voyaging / the shrooms so we can dream
Draw is for the sedation when dreams need settling
Ketamine's to get you out of body / and out of skin
The amphetamine's for unfettering the energies
Speed for the fatigue at the end of the week
Cos we're tired but can't stop / we're dying but alive
We're wired but empty and we're too young to fight
Cos we're tired but can't stop / we're dying but alive
We're young but we can't dance 'til we're high

I trace a path across the carcass of the nightlife
City changing with the first shades of daylight
The dawn spills over the streets / it pains my eyes
Like the sight of suits and shopkeepers putting up signs
They look at us like who are these freaks?
We've got our hoods up and saucer eyes turned to our feet

We have to hurry home / before reality catches up and
takes away the buzz and leaves us with nothing
Oh my God / we're living dead / so many miles to tread
The music's still ringing in my head and it's killing me
Oh my Days / is this Park Street still? / another never-ending hill
I'm on my last quarter pill getting shivery
Oh my skull is full of Oh my gosh / I'm pulling
one last step / like swimming in cement as it sets around my soul
I need a zoot and a cup of tea and a fucking sea of mattresses

we're coming down / one by one
we fall / one by one / we fall...

Cos the beer is for the friendship / whisky's for the winter freeze
Poppers are for the comeup / wallet's for the entry fees
Ecstasy's for the love, passion and depression
Viagra is for fucking / vodka's for forgetting
The cocaine is for the self-esteem
The acid's for the voyaging / the shrooms so we can dream
Draw is for the sedation when dreams need settling
Ketamine's to get you out of body / and out of skin
The amphetamine's for unfettering the energies
Speed for the fatigue at the end of the week
Cos we're tired but can't stop / we're dying but alive
We're wired but empty and we're too young to fight
Cos we're tired but can't stop / we're dying but alive
We're young but we can't dance 'til we're high

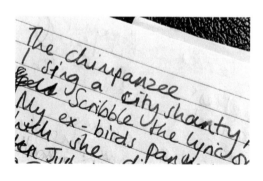

# EXPLODING SLOWLY
2009-2015

June 2009. Blog. Brighton.

a holy week in the studio, writing and recording...

We were in the Zu in Lewes, by the riverside, a big broad room full of sofas and parachutes hanging. It was our home and workplace, the music factory where we slept and laughed lots of laughter.

While next door, a very real factory churned out noises from morning 'til 4.30pm, making recording during the day impossible. We'll just adjust our body clocks then, said we. And the nights became our domain. Coming out to smoke by the river at 3am, watching the Tesco night workers move around their offices in the striplighting, on the other bank.

The tracks are sounding mad, beautiful... an apt reflection of the week that was. Doors crashing shut, violins, kids singing outside, kora, bells and silver balls, me twatting a skip... all these feature on the songs. I need a few days off to regroup the army of crazies in my head, and then we'll get to work on the finishings... I plan to have the album done by August, and there'll be a proper launch in the autumn. Working title? 'Engurland (City Shanties)'.

# Engurland (City Shanties)
Dizraeli / CommUnity Sounds (2009)


## HOMEWARD BOUND
## (ON THE OVERGROUND)

[ *atmos : Laura running on pebbles, Brighton beach* ]

*...aren't you coming in?*

*I'm going down, my boys, to old Maui*
*To the town of the broad brown sea*
*I'm homeward bound on the overground*
*Going down to old Maui....*
*... to old Maui.*

*(hello. My name's Terry*
        *I'm here to fuck with your head*
                        *shall we get started?)*

# TO THE GARDEN

*Garden made of snow*
*Nothing living lies below*
*Hear the songbird breathing slow*
*In a garden made of snow...*

One quarter of the muddy platoon man
And I'm not in it for the drugs and the poontang
Release songs like they're coloured balloons man
See them rise 'til they bump on the moon landscape,
I'm rooted but my heads in the clouds though
Etch a message in indelible sound bro
My letters spread around the globe like Katrina did
Anti-hurricane, cos I build where my thesis hits.
But still a storm, you can't shutter me in voodoo
Must travel like Huckleberry Finn used to
Sketch a picture of your mum in a tin tutu
just to confuse you
Then I make a tune for your buttocks and hips to move to
Let your buttoned-up lips get loose through the process
No need for the singer mate
I speared Britney, then I peed in the Timberlake
Finally a little peace from the scrilla game
The emp-TV screen, and the titty shake
Zim Zimmer / frame / I ate the keys to your Bimmer
Lay by from the speed of the interstate

*In a garden, made of sand*
*Mona Lisa leads the band*
*They strike up when she lifts her hand*
*In a garden made of sand...*

I'm loving this, it's brilliant when my friends are round me
Without breaking objects, we break boundaries
...at times we do break objects, and somebody calls the state mounties
But generally, we make sounds with our mouthpieces
It's brilliant... the fact that these scriptures even at times
Make it onto CD's is double D wicked     PROBLEMATIC
Like when you nuzzle the sweet tits of your lover
And each minute fills infinity's limits:
It's bountiful / The beautiful views of the town I hang around, it's cool
Sometimes, I bike out to the Downs and lounge in full
Sunshine. This one time, I stripped down to my bouncy balls,
Browned it all off in the sun, then cooled off in a trout pool
That's it. At least it's what I feel I'm looking for:
The flow of Qi and peace of which you read in Buddhist thought
... but it's rawer than that. It's the gaps between the teeth of the deepest
sea creatures /
attacking squid with black ink and lidded jaws
It's the pitted paw of the jackal / the livid roar of the grizzled bear
The armpit itch of the poet / and it's all sitting there
Blood, stones, sticks, soil
while you're sat listening to Chris Moyles

*In a garden made of worms*
*New Domestos kills the germs*
*Press-ups make your pickle firm*
*In a garden made of worms.*

# ENGURLAND

Skin cancer costs an arm and a leg man
People on the beach self-harming to get tanned
Laid out flat like an army of dead mans
Red necks / red bellies that expand
And contract like jellyfish on the wet sand
Very Engurlish / suncream and sweaty hands
Mingled in with tepid lager / I'm on my 7th can
Can I kick it? Probably not very elegant
Stepping over spaghetti Bacardi Breezer sick
Chilli sauce on my portion of cheesy chips
Silly thoughts / tell a stranger he's a prick
Receive a hit / lips and teeth are split.
But it in't a party unless you bleed a bit
Bit of a geezer, telling Lisa she's a fitty
Grab her tits, and she's throwing a seizure fit
Now I'm sleeping in a cell / police are dicks

*Engurland, mingerland, middle*
*fingerland*
*Footie song singerland*
*Baddiel and Skinner-land*
*School dinnerland*
*Red white, brown and gingerland*
*Imperial hinterland*
*Perpetual winterland*
*Where happy pills are in demand*
*Engurland, engurland, engurland*
*Aren't you proud?*

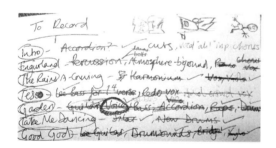

| *I cut the second verse of this one, because it made me squirm in my now-pants with lines about teenage mums and losing your virginity in a carpark that (although they were written about things and people I knew well growing up) just smelled too much of crude fekin stereotypes and I didn't like it.* |

press his button, he collapses like a wood giraffe

# BOMB TESCO

Who's this? Another rapper with a messiah complex
Thinking when I write a concept, it stops the nonsense
But God chuckles, so I let go
Playing African drums in the carpark of Tesco
My heart is vast and growing / it beats in paradiddles
Casting poems out through the drab and the drizzle
that drives down / and penetrates the shoppers' coats
One office bloke gives me a look like
"you can't stop this bro"...
But I can bang a drum until my hands fall apart
And if it makes one shopper dance,
that's my calling answered
My reason for playing the evening 'til the morning after
Carry my flame like stigmata through the falling darkness
and the rising light—I hit the goatskin
The nature of sound means it always finds an opening
This time, I'm hoping it might find your lugholes
And if it does, I'll flood your subconscious with a drumroll...

*That's the movement, what?*
*The movement*
*None of your rulers can stop the movement*
*Because it moves in the veins of the movers*
*Their brains and their boots and the strains of their music...*

*("this is your time... Bomb Tesco")*

That's my primal ish, son
My tribal rhythm bounces
Somewhat manically in the cavity of your sinuses
In order to fill your mind with this ethereal medicine
You might just find yourself beatboxing in the cereal section
or tapping 4/4 beats on tins of corned beef
or slapping a solo on a slab of mature cheese
The manager's called Steve,
and he comes over to chat to you
Saying, "please do not practice drum patterns
on cans of tuna
It's very distracting to the consumer"
...but in mid-opus, Steve freezes
and his eyes switch focus
He grabs a pack of Kit-E-Kat and starts to shake a latin rhythm with it
and the shelf-stacker, Dave, is rapping bits of lyrics
...he's very gifted. And within a minute
Delores from storage has chipped in with a sung chorus
in Zulu. They never knew she could do that, it's hard to believe
Steve is beating the bass on two vats of margarine
and Dawn, from customer services, is busting verses
over the P.A., and Gary
who has a nervous twitch, and a weak brain
is stamping out the hardest beats on the counter of the pharmacy
Scattering paracetamol rather anarchically...
Before long, the whole supermarket's deep with raw song
Somebody's even found some frozen cod they can play chords on.
Four long hours later, you step out in the fading light
with a new perception of space and time.
In the carpark, a strange guy is playing a djembe...
what a weird way to waste a Wednesday.

*That's the movement, what?*
*The movement*
*None of your rulers can stop the movement*
*Because it moves in the veins of the movers*
*Their brains and their boots and the strains of their music...*

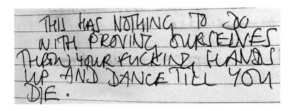

## TAKE ME DANCING

*Take me, take me dancing*
*Take me from this place where I can't even breathe*
*Take me, take me dancing*
*Got no-one to pray to... I'm on my knees.*

*Sail, sail away now*
*And when you sail away let me aboard*
*Cos I am tired, tired of running*
*Tired of screaming, and I'm tired of being ignored.*

# GOOD GOD

[ *atmos : street preacher, Brixton tube station* ]

For my mate Mike, God is called Christ
It gives him headspace among the highrises
Lends order to the muddle of his mind,
Sorts his troubles into sins
Helps him struggle through a crises.
For Tom-Tom, God is Dionysis
...he prays by dropping little white hits
And waits for the hurricane of light
Blowing rugged in his eyes
Leaving puddles in his irises
For Polly, God is called Isis:
She steals kisses from the night's lips
Her heart's large enough to hold the moon
She's the chorus of a soul tune
Says a little prayer like this:

*Deep in the belly, you've got to watch what you worship*
*Chasing pennies is a very weird way to find a purpose*
*Get yourself a good god and get yourself free*
*What you call it makes no bones to me*

No bones and no idols, I circle with the cycles
Instrumentals are my temples and the mind is my Bible
I keep it wide open, let my verse flow free
Psalms spoken as an urgent poetry
Words are muscles, and they break commandments

Casting them aside
To let the spark of life set the dark alight
Far and wide over land and sea,
My magic speaks with the thousand mouths of the banyan tree
With all the twisted tongues that nature gives it
Without the grandiose pantyhose of the mystic
Who sacrifices sense at an altar shrine:
"the body's sinful and the soul's divine"
Well, I've had a skinful of an older wine
I came free, now I'm going forth and multiplying
The same beast that was present at the origin of people
I'd rather one tree than a forest of cathedrals...

*Deep in the belly, you've got to watch what you worship*
*Chasing pennies is a very weird way to find a purpose*
*Get yourself a good god and get yourself free*
*What you call it makes no bones to me.*

# IT WON'T BE LONG

One time for your crooked mind, said I
As I gave the man a pound
He said, "thank you stranger
The deed will come back round;
Perhaps we'll drink together, man
Next time you pass through town"
Picks up his guitar again and sings:

*It won't be long before I'm gone*
*Swallowed by the road I lie upon*
*It won't be long before I'm gone*
*Swallowed by the road*
*I stumble on*

*...there's no backing down.*

Two times for your crooked mind, said I
As I gave the man coin
He said, "I don't need money now
But I could smoke a joint"
"Fine", said I
Sat by his side
I rolled and rolled, he told his life
And toked like he deserved to choke
And die...

He said

*It won't be long before I'm gone*
*Swallowed by the road I lie upon*
*It won't be long before I'm gone*
*Swallowed by the road*
*I stumble on*

*...there's no backing down.*

Three times for your crooked mind
Standing at the grave.
Many of us fall
And very few are saved
It makes no difference now,
If he cursed, or if he prayed
Perhaps we'll drink together
One of these days...

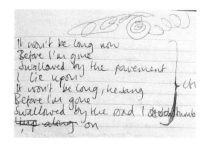

# REACH OUT

| *I have a treasured friend who is a sex worker. So I have blacked out the word 'whores'.*
*It's blind and clumsy and has been used as a weapon.* |

Old man creeps in the streets in the puddles
Holds down the need to speak of his troubles
Both hands shake with the Parkinson's
that is starting to break him.
Darkening sun sets over the streetlights—a night with no stars in
One shadowy figure steps into a doorway
Where the ████ play the same games as always.
The old man's seen it all before, he could tell you some morbid stories
He's been through four wars and one divorce,
Carries a twitch that he got from the Blitz
He's had a lifelong lover lost to the void
He's seen his brothers destroyed
by the tick tock Bang Bang of reality
... just another picture to hang in the gallery.

*You need to reach out*
*Into the darkness*
*Before it reaches you.*

Old man sits on train as it rumbles
Over land soaked in rain and struggle
...the motion of it shakes his brain in a muddle
like Boggle dice contained in a bubble.
Man stops at stops in his pub crawl
in villages, on grubby stools.

He grins and orders in house double
No rocks in it—got to sort out his own rubble
His mind is full of mumbles: a jar full of colour
in among bubblegum fools
None of these suckers get him. Numbness sets in
Turns his stride to a stumble,
Tripping over his feet, back to the train
Rain seeps through cracks in the pane
Window frames him: too old a man for a salary
...just another picture to hang in the gallery.

*You need to reach out*
*Into the darkness*
*Before it reaches you.*

# MARIA

He sits with his head in his hands
His feet sunk into the sand
The sky turns grey above him;
He shows no sign of being alive.
But what can a boy do?
The day the world went wrong
he was in the front row.
What must he go through to pay, to pay?
Well, he don't know
Maria was his sweetness, his light
his redress, his night, his day
They rented a flat together and shared the summer
in their hideaway.
All he needed was her cheek pressed to his
and his world was calm.
He could almost weep
watching her sleeping
in the circle of his arms.

There was one day they woke up early
and the dawn was splashed with gold.
Maria jumped up and wanted to walk
in the morning cold
so they left, undressed
and stepped outside
strode the avenues
nude and giggling
unashamed, and unafraid of any truths

the universe may cast their way,
whatever time may bring
they danced among the city greys and
then he heard her sing...

*Won't you follow me*
*And find a space a little closer to the sea*
*To float away away away*
*Today today today today...*

But then the seasons spun
The weakened sun began to fade
with such freedoms come poverty
and food has to be paid for.
Maria was too much a wild child to work for living
so it was he who went out chasing papers, while she
chased her visions.
Imprisoned in suits and factory uniforms
He slaved to pay for them both, dawn through to dawn
through to dusk. Resentment cultivated into mistrust
in his mind, and nothing hits us like a kiss does
when there's very little love left within it
and workaday stress had stretched his love to its limits
Money makes money, somebody said
but the money he made barely bought bread
for the table, and when you watch the weeks tick away
and the clock on the factory wall steals the day
and all that's left you is the grey of twilight
and the long tired nights
there's got to be a point
when your fire dies.

His was fading fast;
No number of Maria's laughs could warm him
Someone should have warned him
Even a crack in the design can let a storm in
and the architecture of their love
was looking worn thin.
A smile, a worried glance, an angry thought.
A fumbled coffee cup, a slap, a slammed door
She wanted to make love
He needed to sleep
She wanted to talk
He thought she thought too deep
When she sang

*Won't you follow me*
*And find a space a little closer to the sea*
*To float away away away*
*Today today today today...*

And to his mind it seemed that
Maria'd lost her rhyme and her reason
In her drinking and daydreaming.
Sick of coming home to the mess she made with
scattered sculptures, and fragments of scribbled pages
She called it art—
he called her from work and said he'd be home late.
Needed some of his own space
Needed a drink. He went with a couple of work mates
to a bar just opened close to the factory gates
and his mates were chatting about these women they find fit
Saying they wouldn't mind a bit of it

**Ed.**
**12:01 PM 11 Jul**

the blonde here seems to fall
into the camp of demonic
temptress trope rather than
human female. with that and
the name 'maria' we've got
a madonna / whore thing
going on. not sure how i feel
about it. how much are Maria
and the blonde symbols vs
people? what does this song
mean to you?

**Rowan Sawday**
**3:12 PM 11 Jul**

Yes really good point - this
song is a v old one (written
in 2005) and I've performed
it so many times that it's
become just noises really. It's
such a favourite of people's
that I think it should be
included, and i'd like to write
something acknowledging
these boil-in-a-bag Woman
Tropes. I think that's a better
thing to do than to exclude
the piece. I was listening
to an Octavia Butler essay
which she'd gone back into
and put a load of side-notes
into, things she would have
written differently now etc; I
really liked the honesty and
integrity of that

Considering

and in the midst of it

our friend was drunken-hypnotised

by this blonde bit of skirt

with cute little eyes

that flickered like the serpent's tongue

      blatantly flirting

He thought, just what i need after a week's working

And

*one drink leads to another thing*

*he finds himself pressed against the barside fumbling*

*with this blonde bird*

*mumbling something about*

*going back to hers*

*and before he knows*

*she's pulling off her skirt.*

*three hours later*

*it's long done and over*

*in his sleep, becoming*

*just a little more sober*

*he's locked within a dark dream*

*in his imagining*

*he's scrabbling to find Maria*

*but she keeps vanishing*

he woke, cold and shaking

in a sudden sweat

driven by fear, he rushed to gather up

his stuff and left

running with his head spinning
his tongue raw
running through the streets that had been theirs
the summer before
he reaches the door of the flat and tiptoes in
hoping to find his lover there, soft and dozing
but there was no lover, no sound
no smiles
just Maria's artwork, stacked
in neat little piles.

He burst into the bedroom
but she wasn't there
just a rumpled pillow
and a strand of her hair.
And a note
where she would have laid her head
and the moment that he saw it
he knew that she was dead.
It read

*Won't you follow me?*
*And find a space a little closer to the sea*
*To float away away away*
*Today today today today...*

*And everything must die*
*No sooner dry than we are taken by the tide*
*And float away away away*
*So very little time to play*

If you observe an ordinary object or body very closely, it is transformed into something sacred.

— ISABELLE ALLENDE

# White Man (Moves)
Dizraeli & Tom Caruana (2013)

*Hello, man-boy. Take a trip to India, then overland from India to London through Iran, Turkey, Europe. And answer this: How do you write yourself and your experience as a white grandson of Empire (your great-great-grandad was a missionary in Mysore; your grandad was posted to India in the war; your dad was born in Kashmir) without some missteps, or skirtings unsettlingly close to the Bones?*

*Looking back at the songs of this album now, I see the answer is, 'you don't.'*

*But I want to include some of these lyrics anyway, because I think they are useful in showing a descendent-of-colonisers' attempts to understand his relationship with all that history; with the injustices he perceives here and now as he makes his own White Man Moves.*

*Reading the lyrics of this album a decade later, what do I see? I see I was critical of other travellers' blindnesses without being conscious enough of my own; that I was flying my own little White Saviour flag without even noticing; I could go on and on but that's enough.*

*Here are some lyrics from a thing I made ten years ago. They are full of holes. I hope they speak with you.*

# AZIM

[ *atmos : busy street, Chennai* ]

Azim drives a rickshaw / Azim's dreams are limitless
Azim fiends for Englishness / wait 'til his MBA finishes
He'll pedal his rickshaw to Paris with his / sensible trousers
And his impeccable manners / and Azim drives a rickshaw
He's pisspoor / really can't afford the supper he's forking out for
For who though? He's paying for you and me hun
Us two muggy muddy-headed couple of heathens
Who shoot looks at each other struggling for reasons
Why anybody would do something so decent.
Azim folds his napkin / Azim doesn't drink,
Pushes out chair, stands and gives a sudden glimpse
Of a vast-hearted, grand-mannered, stubborn-chinned
Son of 600 years of shit-shovelling underlings
Azim conjures wonderment
No pot to piss in / Stop though. Shit Ro.
My wallet's missing...

# WHAT RIVER IS THIS?

Tell me if you can, what river is this?
A cracked gully, a gutter, a trickle of piss
Crow catches Rat and picks at his ribs
And on the banks, what once were villagers live
Fine spot for a match of cricket is this
Here where the noon sun blisters your lips
And the houses are rags, and splinters of sticks
And the kids' bones are toothpicks for the rich
This is the hole where India shits
Even the train tracks give it a miss
And the sea shudders to think of its kiss
White man, that's the kind of river this is

*Tell me if you can*
*Just tell me if you can (taking a train)*
*Tell me if you can*
*Tell me if you can (taking a train)*
*(Taking a train, taking a tr-)*

Tell me then, friend, what government's this?
Sleeping in the shade with its guns at its hips
Head resting on the bundle that is bloody and ripped
Belly pushing out under the jut of his ribs
Because his unpaid wage has him hungry for tips
Like the truckers at the picket line, wanting a lift
And the slum kids hunting for a pocket to pick
And all the others that have felt the thud of his stick

This government sleeps by a puddle of spit
Crimson and white, like a skull crushed with a brick
But once he cried out of love for his kids
Understand, ill is what this government is

*Tell me if you can (tell me if you can)*
*Tell me if you can (tell me if you can)*
*Tell me if you can (tell me if you can)*
*Tell me if you can (tell me if you can)*

*[ atmos : dictaphone recording, Kerala to Delhi train ]*

*...They've got begging bowls balanced on the spheres of their stomachs / here the*
*injustice is as fierce as the sun is /*
*So it's just as inevitable here as the hundreds of weird*
*motherfuckers with beer in their tumblers*
*who say, "Isn't poverty fascinating?"...*

# PEOPLE TAKING PICTURES

Conspicuously pale-faced, solitary soul
Dressed western in a city that could swallow me whole
Try not to catch the eye of the money patrol
Looking at me like my body's made of dollars and gold
I Am Rich / Scan my pockets for bulges
My cockiness is false, my wallet is swollen
I fumble your currency like Monopoly notes
And spend your week's wage on a bottle of coke

One of the people taking pictures
of the people taking pictures
of the people from the pictures of the people.
The people make a face
to put the people in the picture
that the picture of the people isn't real.
But to the people taking pictures
nothing matters but the pic
to put the people in the picture back at home
Picture it: "look at the people in the picture.
So *Real!*"
...make the picture wallpaper on your phone.

I buy mineral water, and sweat it away.
See the confetti petals match the red of my face
Stepping in pace to the drums the percussionists play
The only White Man in your wedding parade
Men like me from Tibet to Mesopotamia
look for realness as a method of escape:

Dumbstruck among beggars and stray dogs
I came cos I relish the chaos

But I became a person taking pictures
of the people taking pictures
of the people from the pictures of the people.
The people make a face
to put the people in the picture
that the picture of the people isn't real.
But to the people taking pictures
nothing matters but the pic
to put the people in the picture back at home
Picture it: "look at the people in the picture.
So *Real!*"
...make the picture wallpaper on your phone.

As I sip a Kingfisher, in Pasha
in passionate chatter with a man,
Pat (whose hair's matted)
I say, "yes mate. But if the chess game's
Universal, shouldn't we let the rest play?
like Ganesh, Lolla and
Parvita, who
came to the beach to do
selling, cuz they need a few
pennies, and they shake
necklaces and bangles
like a prisoner
shakes chains on his ankles
saying

"please come buy,
sir, madam, please"
...to the beach bums frying
in factor fifteen
sun grease, Pat
and I have to come clean
Pat.
I'm ashamed to be named as one of these...

people taking pictures
of the people taking pictures
of the people from the pictures of the people.
The people make a face
to put the people in the picture
that the picture of the people isn't real.
But to the people taking pictures
nothing matters but the pic
to put the people in the picture back at home
Picture it: "look at the people in the picture.
So *Real!*"
...make the picture wallpaper on your phone.

jesus wept, damien cooed, the crowd unpeeled and went away.

# PICKING THROUGH THE PEBBLES

There used to be a waterfall here
It leapt out the rocks with a yell
People used to come from all over
just to camp close to where the water fell
But then the government banned falling
And the cascade shrank to a stream
Reduced to two pipes and one gutter
Just enough to wet the mud to a dull gleam
But still the officials felt threatened
So they built little walls to hold the water in
Now the two pipes piss into a puddle
that's occasionally ruffled by the wind
But this couple still come to take pictures
And they look up at the hills in the hope it's snowed
and swap stories of the old river
while their son looks through the pebbles for a stone to throw

Picking through the pebbles
Picking through the pebbles
Picking through the pebbles for a stone to throw
Picking through the pebbles
Picking through the pebbles
Picking through the pebbles for a stone to throw
Picking through the pebbles
Picking through the pebbles
Picking through the pebbles for a stone to throw
Picking through the pebbles
Picking through the pebbles
Picking through the pebbles for a stone

Mohammed knows what it means to dance dreams
and they couldn't dam his flow cos it's flooding through his arteries
And he closes curtains / but he won't close his arms please
Have you heard the volume of his heartbeat?
He's a wardrum and he's got friends the same as him
Immense / irrespective of attempts to cage 'em in
Young proud Iranians / who said the music died?
A million Mohammeds kept the roots alive
Listen: they fed it whisky and illicit tunes
and it grew by the light of a strobe in the living room
Angular / angry / broad-leaved enough to catch the screams of
*I love this fucking TUNE*

Picking through the pebbles
Picking through the pebbles
Picking through the pebbles for a stone to throw
Picking through the pebbles
Picking through the pebbles
Picking through the pebbles for a stone to throw
Picking through the pebbles
Picking through the pebbles
Picking through the pebbles for a stone to throw
Picking through the pebbles
Picking through the pebbles
Picking through the pebbles for a stone

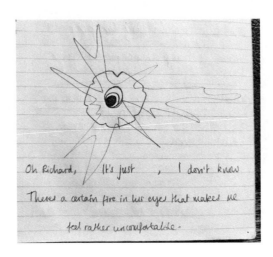

Oh Richard, / It's just , I don't know
There's a certain fire in his eyes that makes me
feel rather uncomfortable.

## FORWARDS

My companion and I / travelling the desert line
Cross camelback hills rising like a leather spine
Forwards / keep on forwards / shift forwards / keep on forwards
Northwest borders / Qazvin to Tabriz
Snowswept orchards / tracks seem to track me
Forwards keep on forwards / shift forwards keep on forwards
Attaturk-ish men at the crossroads / and the dervish spins like a top thrown
There's a Kurdish boy selling tissues / the hospital overflows with his relatives
You and me are on the slow coach / struggling muddy roads
The women's hair is suddenly uncovered / so gorgeous
The valley turns moon-silver / the hills throw rubble but the bus still lurches
Forwards still forwards keep forwards shift on forwards
*Move*

# WHITE STONES

*white stones in the valley of the butterflies*
*stoned in the butterfly land*
*bleached bones in the bottom of the valley in the sun*
*white stones in the cup of my hand*
*white stones in the valley of the butterflies*
*bones where the tigerbird lands*
*stoned by the opium of ocean in the sun*
*captured in the valley I am*

*I've never been so sober white tiger*
*I've never been so sober white tiger*
*I've never been so sober white tiger*
*night-flyer good night to ya*
*light fire for ya*

3rd August

Lost focus at some point and ended up on the roof, London beetling below.

An attack inevitable, a question of when not if.

# Moving in the Dark
Dizraeli & The Small Gods (2013)

*[ atmos : bunyip emerging breathless from underwater ]*

## WE HAD A SONG

The universe was a fresh place
We sucked it up as much as possible
Never dug on rock n roll much
With us it's all
decks trucks and hospitals
Drugs and drum n bass
carried us, lifted off the buzz of jungle raves
Bosh chemical cudgels for the added feeling
White boys pirating the culture of the Caribbean
Can of Red Stripe from the Bedmi Asda
The bass is the bollocks; the drop is the viagra
Cos we felt hard as fuck, boxing the air
Bopping in circles
Taxing cigarettes, clocking the girls
Hadn't figured yet the world is complex, disordered
All we had to do was learn the rules and we'd be sorted...

None of us had died at that time. That was before Nick
Before the fit before his birthday.
Before Hakkan
Before the earthquake

We are the last
two survivors
All the lights are
out.
We find each other
in the dark.

Before the funerals
Before hindsight made them all beautiful
And gave us all stopwatch eyes, like
Who'd have thought
we'd be standing here in suits we don't suit at all
who could have known? But still, nobody cry
Instead, grow fears that keep us turning over at night
unable to keep still. Nobody cry:
grief solidifies into meaning over due time
Funny innit? How even good memories hurt
We had a song. I wish I could remember the words.

So can't you see it bruv, I'm made of deeper stuff
I'm made of skateboards, bongs and Sega beat 'em ups.
I'm made of binbags stacked high for ollying
I'm made of vert, and the gut-rush from dropping in
And maybe vodka from the Hotwells Road Spa
Panda Pops, Curly-Wurlies and soap bar
I'm made of grip tape and piss takes and broken arms
I'm made of concrete and doner meat and open hearts
I'm made of lost tapes
I'm made of lost mates I made in the days
When I could barely cut the crossfade
And all the lost tapes
And all the lost mates I made in the days
When I could barely cut the crossfade
And bruv we could've kept on it but it went dark
Some of us fell off and some fell apart
But none of us forgot and Nick never died
Cos as long as we're remembered we are kept alive.

# WAS A RAPPER

*There was a rapper in Bristol town who told a wicked story*
*He said "I pray to the ghosts in my head and they speak what lies before me*
*I mould them thoughts into golden orbs and the audience applauds me"*
*And he loved the love of strangers well, but he loved his missus poorly*

*It weren't too long 'til a man ran along and said I'll be your agent*
*They rode to a tower where the cocaine flowed and the fat controller praised him*
*His lady called from home and said that's cause for celebration*
*But he never got back that month he went on tour and kept her waiting*

*There is a pub down Easton Way where tired folk can gather*
*They tell tall tales of a ship full sail and a bold and broken rapper*
*Who went too far too fast in the game where snakes sell broken ladders*
*The ghosts fell out of his head and soon his mind went tumbling after*

*There was a rapper in bristol town but now he begs for coppers*
*Shakes his tin at the spinning door of the fat controller's office*
*Curses all the folk within*
                                    *you fat cunts all are tossers*
*And his girl's long gone, her old love done. She had some better offers*

*There was a rapper in Bristol town who told a wicked story*
*I never had his fame but now I'm glad he lived it for me*
*He died this morning, pulled from the gorge—a sad and listless body*
*Who loved the love of strangers well, but he loved his missus poorly*

# MOVING IN THE DARK

The kiddy to your left / wishes he was white
And he's very jealous of the kiddy to your right
Who wishes he was brown / and fishes for applause
Cracking witticisms / splitting metaphors
For that girl Alice / leggy clever clogs
Who's a bit embarrassed that her voice is very posh
So she tones it down / makes it proper street
Papa would be shocked that she drops T's
Drops E's / drop comes and they jiggle like a loon
Shaking out shapes to the wiggle of the tune
What a pickernick of humans / spillikany mess
Kiddie to your right / kiddy to your left
Pick a head, pick a spindly spillikan and guess
What heart is it / that is sitting in his chest
Pick one Mr Architect / disregard the rest
Ask your questions / try cast the net

Who's that moving in the dark do you see him
Wolf man boogie man queer man human being
Who's that moving in the dark does you hear em
Fox woman ~~daggertooth dog~~ dogheart daggertooth fool
Who's that moving in the black wood clearing
Conquest pindoof pioneer fool
Who's that moving with his mind full of sea
No man no man its only me.

*Who's that moving in the dark?*
*Who's that moving in the dark?*
*Who's that moving in the dark?*
*Who's that moving in the dark?*
*Me man it's me man it's only me*

You've never known anything half as deep as
The place Mark harbours secrets
Sitting in the bath he feeds hemp seeds to his penis
And calls it Big Bad Keith and that's deep
But still isn't as weird as the dreams Lizzie has
'Bout the valley of the broad green lily pads
And the sugar trees growing piggy carcasses
Rotting udders milked by midget gardeners
With dartboards for eyes and birds on leashes
The gardeners will die if the birdsong ceases
And that's deep
But no deeper that the pit he's stuck in
And the fact he's busy fucking Lizzie's husband
That's why he holds Lizzie's hand tightly
Turn our insides out we are unsightly
So don't claim lofty morals mister mighty
The only gods round here sit beside me

# STRONG BRIGHT

On my front step at gone midnight
Overhead, pinprick stars emit a dim light
I watch a late worker scuttle home in his pinstripes
It's the single time I take the space to think wide
so I'm smoking.
Blowing smoke rings at the world in general
London in particular:
the town I've settled in where definitions blur
and the roots of history are disinterred
by rushed spirits driven urgent by the desire to finish first:
The Big Smoke
I add my little cloud to it

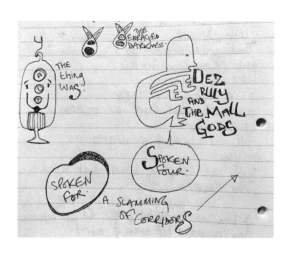

Standing on the Brixton kerb addled by the loud music
playing in my skull
desire to perform
astonish an audience
a fire in a storm cup...
Why I'm needing calm
Hashish is my needle in the arm
It's a fact I breathe deeper when the balm hits
Not gods, we're plasticine people from the tar pits
clod-brains, not conceiving of the vastness
we'll not change. We'll not stop 'til we end
the same way we came: chaos and incomprehension
The Big Bang. I add my little sound to it
I sing positive
when I get around to it
Think I am a good man
but I'm not sure yet
wrapped in a jacket and a towel on the doorstep
earning pay packets from the vowels in my cortex
hooting at the moon with the owls 'til the dawn sets

*Strong, bright*
*Step with all my pride screwed on tight*
*Check, I'm just like you*
*I'm not right in the noggin but I persevere*
*Spanners in my engine*
*but I'm managing pretending I am*
*Strong...*

They tell me pain makes for good writing / Grey days and
neighbourhood violence / razor blades and military mindsets
I'm sick and I'm tired of it / I revel in my difference
I'm spending my time with kiddies from all walks of life and I'm
listening / Never denied the plain fact I ain't black and I'm
middle class / fed up of guys that change accents
and play twat to spit a bar / Rappers stabbing everything
in sight, it's uninspiring / Saying they're handling more long hoes
than firemen / What insight is there there? They're unprepared
/ for the fact that if you act hard you miss the fun of the fair
In deep depression / I'm doing the Lambada in my underwear
in the freezer section / with a finger puppet on my erection /
Fucking Yeah / Release the pressure like a lifted lid / If you're
gifted it's sufficient no need to play the victim, Tim / or turn
the crucial fact to crucifiction / I'm through with bitching /
do whatever you do to fit in / But stay

*Strong, bright*
*Step with all your pride screwed on tight*
*Check, I'm just like you*
*I'm not right in the noggin but I persevere*
*Spanners in my engine*
*but I'm managing pretending I am*
*Strong...*

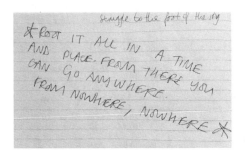

*struggle to the foot of the sky*

✱ Root it all in a time
and place. From there you
can go anywhere.
From nowhere, nowhere ✱

# NEVER MIND

*Nod your heads like they're hitting the wall....*

You might see me walking round with a slight limp
It's not a G thing bruv – I've done my ankle in
A bit thrown like the dice in the I Ching
I'm not sleeping well, my head is tangling
I need an aspirin bruv I need a Saturday
A cup of tea to drink, possibly a Jaffa Cake
Or just an evening alone
I've had a manic day
It's been an age since I was chilled enough to mastur...
Baby! Come here, I love you, you're my stinky tits
You could help me with my problem come to think of it
Rinky dink? Sugar plum? Twinkle clit?
I didn't mean stinky tits..! Sorry. I've been a dick
Sorry! Sorry...
That was worse than dreadful
It's my stress levels,
It's my work schedule

At my desk, headful of words
Unsettled, unearthed
I'm Dizzy, I'm in effect
I'm ineffectual / but come on...

*Never mind, it doesn't matter what you look like*
*All that matters is you dance*
*Cos it's a very very short life.*

I move fast
All the flies on me are blue-arsed
The kid that turned pages 'til he got to the rude part
and hit the kerbs naked with a sock on his doo-dah
It's a wonderful night for a moon dance.
Cherubims serenade us on a sketchily-tuned harp
Venus plays a bass string strung between two starts
Jesus levitates on a fungus with blue hearts
and Sarah Palin's abducted in Utah...
"pardon?"
I said welcome to the Terrordome
Never give acid to a man with a megaphone
He will get frantic and then he won't let it go
Have you ever seen a rapper's head explode?
ROLL UP!!
And when the crowd dies
I hope that they've been entertained
and found me useful. Like safety information on a train
Cos to be truthful, I craved just a little taste of fame
Then it hit me – ego is a waste of brain

*So*
*Never mind, it doesn't matter what you look like*
*All that matters is you dance*
*Cos it's a very very short life.*

# SAILOR

*I wish I were a sailor on the sea*
*With all the seabirds flying after me*
*The sun would alter course on my decree*
*If I were a sailor*

Please trust me
You can't trust me
I wear a hat to bed and the inside of my head's ugly
You don't want me - you want the other me
From the stage portrayal
You are chasing vapour trails
Real Me rolls with a crew of One multiplied
Bedfellows with a stupid drunk poltergeist
Fucking up my workspace
But he's writing all my rhymes for me
My life is borderline tawdry
Caught in my story, you don't wanna be a chapter
I'm a bunch of wankers, only one of me's a rapper
Course I'm just the man to be your skinny dip companion
Capable of dancing with a limited abandon
But my looks of love are a shallow as a grave is
I conjure feeling by imagining you naked
I tumble easily in passionate embraces
but once the semen's out I'm dashing for the gate
Or scrabbling for pages to fit this scene
I will turn you into a sick sixteen
with a middle and an ending and a stiff stitched seam
Isn't it amazing where a pissed kiss leads..?

*I wish I were a sailor on the sea*
*With all the seabirds flying after me*
*The stars would alter course on my decree*
*If I were a sailor on the sea*
*I wish I were a rooster on the run*
*My song would chase the shadow from the sun*
*I'd make these young hens mothers every one*
*If I were a rooster*

# WHITE RUM

We made ourselves small last night. Expelled air
Shrunk to a pinprick of starlight
and held there,
Breathless
Suspended in the seas we'd sweated
Time puddled in a deep green second
'Til the phone rang.
I threw it to the wall with both hands
and lay back into you
Tangle of cracks and sinew
so like nothing you could die from it.
Small white hair
on your chin I spotted.
That's the thin line we walk
We roll
We deep talk we
raw sex
We seesaw
'Til the brass balls on your headboard
knock plaster off the wall all of a sudden and we pause
panting. All gape and action
red-rubbed skin we are
all ache and atoms
Suddenly conscious of us
back to base
And love
Is there a contract that states
How much
eye contact to make?

I mean we met last week
and he's back next week
which
sets our scene
to be a short one
Remind me not to fall in
I'm a sucker for shared showers
and slow mornings
And you're so good at that thing
don't stop, love
But love is so not us
So not now
So what do I call you?
When we're moved and the hour's late
I still hide my shoes from your housemates

For heaven's sakes...

But really now

Fuck it
It's good to get to know you so cosy
Fuck it
Missioning alone gets lonely
Good to know you want me
If for sex only
Let's touch toes
see where it goes
Fuck it love
Hold me

But if the phone rings again, the spell's broken.
I'm a touch tired, holding myself open
When I'm sore headed from the time we both spent soaked in
Your sweat, my sweat
and Ted Hughes poems.
Listen- Whatever gets you going
I will do that
Whatever breaks your blocks down
Do that and don't stop now
We are so cock-proud
We can crow 'til we're both knocked out
and wake later
Do it again babe
sorry not babe but I dare not
Say your name
In case of emerging seas
In case of it hurting me
Your death
Falls from your face as an urgent scream
And you spasm in a high fantasm
And you say,
that's the first time that's happened
A new day
Rises over Balham and we both sleep
Tangled in the love that doesn't know me

But really now

Fuck it
It's good to get to know you so cosy

Fuck it
Missioning alone gets lonely
Good to know you want me
If for sex only
Let's touch toes
see where it goes
Fuck it love
Hold me

## MILLION MILES

And I'll come back—if ever I die
Save a place at your table
and we'll drink chat, about the other side
Never think that this is goodbye
Cos we've got something of the divine
When we touch tongues—sinking into silence
Glad though. Take a little time from the mad flow
The clutter of the mind
You're my cradle
Rock me in your arms if you're able
Make my head calm and stable
Although I am a wonderer I need rest
I find it in the space where our cheeks press
Together in the blue and the deepness
Forever you and the ceaseless
rhythm of a heartbeat
Heart beat
Let it all go...

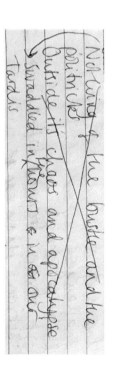

*Cos we're a million years old*
*and we're a billion light years gone*
*and we'll sit till we turn to stone*
*and we will let the globe spin on.*

It's my fortress
Within it we can make love thoughtless
Sweating and moving in a vortex
Nothing in the galaxy matters now
Batten down our shutters in darkness
Swaddled in the hours in our tardis
Invisible and physical—untarnished
Hold both my hands, my lullaby
Butterfly distant from the politricks
Outside it's agony apocalypse
Now the images from the horror flicks
have spilled out the cinemas
War in the schools, war in the bars
Leave it,
whether the weather burns or freezes
It's forever you and the ceaseless
rhythm of a heartbeat
Heart beat
Let it all go...

*Cos we're a million years old*
*and we're a billion light years gone*
*and we'll sit 'til we turn to stone*
*and we will let the globe spin on.*

# TRICK OF THE MOON

what crazy rhythm is this'un / hun please tell me that it isn't
the same rhythm that your face twitches in
you are an obsession / you move like you've got answers
i move like I've got questions / whose music are you dancer?
whose music are you
dancer? whose music do
you dance ta
whose goose would you
let gander?
whose lies will you
ever tanta?
banter doesn't work /
pampering doesn't work /
to her i'm a douchebag
turd / my fantasy grows
like a cancer / on my
nerves / oh my word
my days isn't this true
i'm amoeba with you
i'm a fever with you / feeble prick among you / you like a trick
of the moon / you like a lick of the spoon

*for some reason or other*
*i love her*
*even though she's a nutter*

What a trip that was / look i fell for the moon
slipped up under her / int she's a tricksy customer
all upwards like a buttercup / custard coloured clown
sat up there, waggling her ears / buttering a cloud
here's me tugging her down / my feet stuck in the mud of the
south downs / my tongue in her mouth
hers in my mouth / jiggling about clumsily silly me
silly us trying to make one body from two
isn't feasible is it, is it? / whatever hey diddle diddle we did it
did it / then i played finger fiddle with her cat
and her cat purred her trigger was triggered / so frig it you
know frig it / Isn't every day that you slip in / and get a full lick
of the spoon / In love with a trick of
the moon

*for some reason or other*
*i love her*
*even though she's a nutter*

# THE LITTLE THNGS

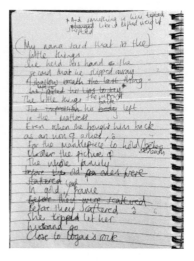

My nana told me it's the little things
She held his hand the second
that he slipped away
and something in him shifted
like a lifted weight
The little things
The imprint his back left in the
mattress
even when she brought him back
as an urn of ashes
for the mantlepiece to hold, beneath
the picture of the whole family
In gold leaf frame, before they scattered
She let her husband go close to Logan's Rock
Waved her sweet heart away and waited for her own to stop
beating
the bottom of the urn till the last burnt
bone cinder fell, she'll tell if you ask her
The little things
She can spin them into epic webs
The waves break stones without diminishing her tenderness
But her address book's filling up with dead friends
Her chest filling with the things she never said to them
The little things
So now the old girl's blatant
You would be too if you had watched the whole world fading

Do with the truth what you will
She'll hold hers blazing
Cancer took her left breast, grandpa took her patience
But no bugger took her pride ever - clear mind
Though she turns a hundred in seven year's time
A century's a whole lot of repetition to live through
A lot of channels of television to flick through
And her limbs function less efficient than they did do
Still it's the little things that stick with you

The little things
The things you never said enough

Things I never said enough:
You're a legend love, keep your centredness, your sense of fun
It's all a goose chase when it's said and done
And you're right, it's all good
as long as you bring your friends along
and they know you as a mate to be depended on
a maker of memories. And yes you were right
It's 20 times better to be loved when you're alive
than idolised by some adolescent sucking egos
I've come a long way since the essence up on East Slope Hill
I get props, still the flexing isn't me though
and I owe that to you - have you read my sleeve notes?
I wrote my gratitude to you there - it's simple
Thank you
I carry you still even now I'm single
Even though I don't roll over for a morning hug and find you
and we were forced to cut the binds we'd tied to
I couldn't find a truth short enough for haiku
so now I'll write a lifetime of Lauras into my tunes

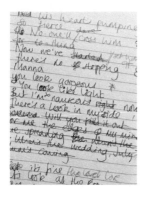

It's all for you
It's really all for you
It's all for you love
It's really all for you
It's all for you
It's really all for you
It's all for you love
It's really all for you
... it's all for you Laura,
True.

Things I never said enough
You're a legend bruv
Keep your dander up, you anchor me
There's no granite tough as love for family
And even if a cancer comes for one of us
the other one will carry on the legacy
We're our daddy's sons
and that's a heavy flag to wave
but look geeze, you're doing it
However many Saturdays you took E's and chewed your lip
Your love's far bigger than the drugs are
Sit and prop up the bar with me
We've been living too quickly.
That's part of the mission innit?
I guess it's alright
but I wish we spent more time.
and Listen
I'm chuffed for you and Miriam
You'll make a lush truth for your kids to live in

and Sorry I never bought a present or sent a card
I meant to
The life I lead's a seven nights a week flipping head screw
But whatever, there's forever shit to get through
Just know how much it is that I respect you

And listen.
It's all for you
It's really all for you
It's all for you bruv
It's really all for you
It's all for you
It's really all for you
It's all for you bruv
It's really all for you

... it's all for you Toby.
True.

The sea.
This great danger laid against the pebbles all the time.

# THE END OF THE WORLD

*Listen my lover / let's make
one thing clear*

*None of us suckers will make
it from here*

*So refill your tumblers and
shuffle up near*

*The end of the world is
coming*

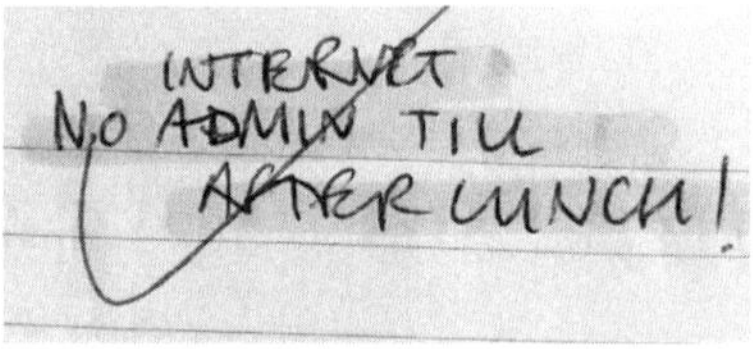
INTERNET
NO ADMIN TILL
AFTER LUNCH!

# Everyone's a Winner - The Mixtape
Dizraeli & DownLow (2013)

[ *atmos : farm dogs and night, Portugal* ]

## RISE

Little balloonatic / you sabre-mouthed dog
Saying how you're pacing round taking out glocks
What about encapsulating You in ways you're proud of?
Shine like the bonnets down at Avonmouth docks
It's a very short existence when you think a minute on it
Some of us sweating / others of us chasing wiggy profits
Summer of recession again
Got a case of shitty Fosters
A case of bollock ache and drug-related willy problems
But we're taking little losses constantly living godless
Some of us rot in civil offices in little boxes
Other of us nibble after-dinner lobsters sipping frosted vodkas
Clinking crystal goblets for the things accomplished
But if you're in, I'm on it / I'm feeling big today
Let's push this flipping lyric business to the limits of it
Let's spray our faith across the city for the kids to clock it
It's not a product it's a little bit of something honest
And that is rarer than you ever would believe bruv
We're sheeped-up / so very many shepherds have deceived us
Fleeced / I'm sick of sheep dip
Please listen these kids have written so much deep shit
You'll drown if you don't perceive it
They're coming close to Jesus

That's the power of proclaiming
The one power that's ours for the taking
That of a thousand ounces of uranium
Contained within the bound'ries of a cranium
So spray it from the mountains or from stadium stages
Say in a blaze of fifty kilowatt lasers
Spill it to the cosmos 'til the gods taste it
You're phosphorescent / volcanic / blow the roof
Give me anecdote so potent mathematics don't compute
The God particle / combined to form compounds
We're lifeforms of electrified water / what now?
Fuck it / let's take it to the outskirts of possible
Galactic anarchy / everybody move your molecules

And rise
keep the moonship rising
must rise
Something has died in your eyes
so come rise
kiddies and creatures alike
the sunrise is frigging godly wonder
these are your times
so come
rise...

Your face holds traces of a truth you carry that I'd love to know
And I wish you'd tell me but I have a hunch you won't
Cos it's safer here innit / hid behind your puppet show
Hunched with your two fists talking and your knuckles broke
love don't protect you but I bet a hundred notes
Punch doesn't get Judy he gets a bloody nose

So maybe just for once sonny give the sun a go
Are you a shooting star, star or a running joke
Dickhead with your swagger and your banner saying drugs are so
Wicked with your mash-up bladder / flaccid as a punctured hope
Huddled in your grubby coat of shivers like it's one below
Saying where's the money mother, where'd the money go?
Nah I'm on a hillock with a gulletful of ones and Oh's
In it Trying to conjure something dope for my countryfolk
Bring it yelling Fuck the front page check your frontal lobes
Check the substances with which they cut your coke
Blood and injustice, and on a another note
son it's summer streak the streets in all your underclothes
Stuff your stomachs speak your piece before the summer goes
Speak your secret griefs in psychedelic colour codes
speak the lions that are lying in your undergrowth
They will keep you flying long after the clubs're closed
Cos you are giants similar to when a sun explodes
And truth has a sledgehammer for your funny bone


Rise
keep the moonship rising
must rise
Something has died in your eyes
so come rise
kiddies and creatures alike
the sunrise is frigging godly wonder
these are your times
so come
rise...

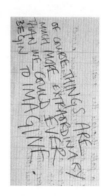

# DO YOU

So back to base / we didn't grow up on an astral plane
We acted waste and went to matches up at Ashton Gate
What a weird way to waste a Saturday
Bongs and bad booze
Sammy got a Bristol City robin tattoo
But what did that prove?
We needed identities / seeded skunk trees and I MC'd
Some of us sold pills / some of us talked shit doubletime
Crew Called Click stepped into sunlight
And some of us spit raps and some of us DJ'd
All of us did tags and tic-tacked to Dean Lane or Skate N Ride
We worshipped Danny Wainwright
We raved nights away and surfaced from the cavelight
Buzzing like a hive of bees in a spinning tempest
Saw in the millenium / ten of us in the city centre
And there were fights everywhere man the shit's relentless
Headless chickens hyped for cockfights, sniff and Bensons
Not Smith and Wessons still tho / this isn't Brooklyn
But you will still get dogged up if you're different looking
I was long haired with paint-spattered cords
They called me jitter still I spat and craved that applause
And the disrespect they gave me only made me practice more
Took some hits to the stomach / became a matador
I mean murker keen learner shirked shifts at BT to be
a proper teamworker
Washing dishes at the hospital
Even served burgers up at Cotham School
Pushed the scene further / never seen a person want it more

We put nights on and time in / and loved it 'til it loved us back
Back before the trendies and the custom caps
I practised up at Cabot Tower cos the wind there makes you feel
X Factor never had the same appeal
Knowing Simon Cowell wouldn't walk in with a major deal
Made us Wu Tang it deeper than a navy seal
think that was Method Man / whatever man it's dopeness
We spoke it 'til we owned it and came back with a depth of focus
Aperture wide open I come with the camera steady
Growing talent and the live hunger that hasn't left me

And I don't promise to be strong but I promise
to be always honest / give you little truths
with the force of prophecy
Seeing all I got is me / and all you've got is you
I speak my life / do what you got to do
And less of the judging
lest you be judged in the same court
for all your flawed sets of assumptions
It's unbecoming
Seeing all I got is me / and all you got is you

I speak my life / Do what you got to do
But do you...

[ DJ DownLow scratch section...]

So who'd have thought?
All the bad kids became the troubadours
Used to fours up fags and
bun a zoot before school started

I s'pose it's all part of growing up
You learn to keep your focus sharp
and your heart closed to love
Foolhardy youngsters
Forever forcing forwards
We craved summers
Maths felt long as August
and August never long enough
I always held onto stuff
too long, whether zoots
or Lauren's love
But first times are hard to best innit boys?
Like the first time I cleared the steps up at Little Lloyds
First time getting past bouncers into sweaty clubs
Necking drugs wishing I was up there where the MC wuz
We bust just becus we must bust it's urgent
Sometimes the fuzz busted us but we'd earned it
Buzzcuts and dusty pumps / fucked trucks and
surf chicks
The first kiss was mucky but the first E was fucking perfect

August
Life was too gorgeous
We carried on
like a tribe of goons lawless
That August
We lost something good that month
But don't look back
Promise
I never looked back once
August

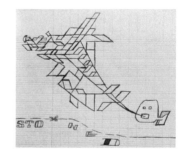

# MINNIE THE MOOCHER (HIDEOUSLY KINKY)

Cab Calloway:
Yo folks here's a story 'bout Minnie the Moocher
She was a low down hoochie coocher
She was the roughest toughest rail
But Minnie had a heart
as big as a whale.

*Hi di hi di hi di hi*
*Ho di ho di ho di ho*
*Hee di hee di hee di hee*
*Hah di hah di hah hi hah*

Give a fuck if you run with a dark army of goons
This my birth song, sung to a daft carnival tune
I am Cardinal Whom / the blue placard marking my home
is hung from the dark part of the moon
I sit on the step stark as a bone
Aardvark in my brain singing Hooray
Swinging a large parcel of stray kittens
I'd rather stay living my insane fiction than yours kiddo
Mine leads to clawed nymphos and robed wrestlers of both sexes
Yours leads to a leap from a tenth floor window
broke necked, with a gram of regret in your nose wretched

*Hi di hi di hi di hi*
*Ho di ho di ho di ho*
*Hee di hee di hee di hee*
*Hah di hah di hah hi hah*

Yih / and I'll probably broil in hell's braziers
But at least in the meantime I'm enjoying myself naked
Oil myself shaped as myself / enough of the self hatred
I've been through the fire five times / been stuck in a cell mate
And there's nothing to tell / fade it
I'm bringing the blitzkrieg
Trying to quiet me nobber? Nibble a ringpiece
Yep / 'til the bigots come lynch me
I'm bringing it stinky
I'm sticking it in deep
From here I'm hideous kinky

*Hi di hi di hi di hi*
*Ho di ho di ho di ho*
*Hee di hee di hee di hee*
*Hah di hah di hah hi hah*
*Poor Min, poor Min, poor Min.*

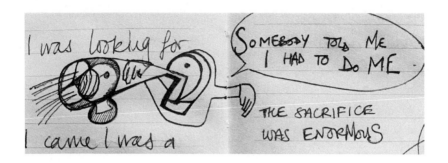

## CUP OF TEA

I dreamed I said I love you / but I didn't dream I meant it
I said it cos you said I'm insufficiently attentive
And I dig you so I promised we'd be digging deeper trenches
Eventually eventually, we'll swim a deeper crevice
It seems I struck a chord that is peanut butter-textured
Sealing shut my jaw and it's blocking up the exits
And now you're leant in, steaming up my lenses
And suddenly I see a stretch of treeless dust and desert
We'll breathe each other's breath
and then we'll preen each other's feathers
Week to week develop the prerequisite resentments
'til we're 61 and 63 and so dependent
that we'll cry each other cups of brine with which to clean our dentures
And I hate it how you pick your feet at breakfast
Your laugh's annoying and your bigotry's offensive
And you're simultaneously sick of me and jealous
to the point I don't allow myself a single female friendship
to the point my head teems with single female wenches

with a penchant for mischievious pensioners
And you were pissed off I never fill the fridge, or clean your dresses
And every Christmas seems to bring a shittier tree of presents
When the mystery has vanished
And I didn't feed your fetish or your fishes
And I never leave you breathless
And I said your niece was weird
And you're pissed off that I said it
And the hiphop that I listen to is for pricks and adolescents
And it's Wednesday and you hate me
And you kiss your teeth and clench
Because I wake you from your daydream
Of hitting me with wrenches
Cup of tea?
                    It's been roughly a century
Since we did any anythings a censor would have censored
Less sensory, more human centipede
I read a book about geese
And sit and watch the tennis
And you hate that, and so do I
I hate tennis
It's senseless
I develop several twitches and attention deficit
And then on a Wednesday we die
And then you're buried
Within an inch of me
Your feet are where my head is
And your head is where my feet are
People stop to read our headstone and say:
"Isn't that sweet, Terrence?"

"That proves love's forever"
Which means relentless
This face I'm making isn't pissy I'm just pensive
Cos my head's as much a mess as our bed is
I said I dreamed I love you
Now I wish I hadn't said it

*Living a lie, living a lie*
*Living a lie 'til the day I die*

# EVERYONE'S A WINNER

Everyone's a winner innit?
Everywhere's a catwalk
Every man's an army, every manhole's a trapdoor
Don't fall in / it gets grizzly
You get a rollerskate / and you get a limousine
It's a right scene innit just?
Live it up a little / bosh a bit of pixie dust
Turn the picture miniature
'Til it's all pocket sized, digestible
Stop look listen / walk where the sign says to walk
Women live by your breasts / men by your testicles
Danger please / keep your legs inside the vestibule

and
scream if you wanna go faster

Rum makes you latin,
Rubber makes you sweat
Tongues are for passion
Lovers are for sex
Love isn't a cuddle
it's a battle to the death
Murk any player who
Rattles your cassette

and
scream if you wanna go faster...

And out of all the mess comes a man without a centre
offering a chemical, it's Satan in his splendour
Saying Saturday it's Saturday a fiver for enjoyment
Your mother's in your mind trying to hide her disappointment

Scream if you wanna go faster

Scrape that barrel babs, your turn to starve now
Walk round begging for a penny with your arse out

Scream if you wanna go faster

The world's made of slavery, gather round your flag
Die very courageously, scratching at your ballbags

Scream if you wanna go faster

There's a war on keep your castle locked
Big house, little house, cardboard box
Big house, little house, cardboard box
Big house, little house, cardboard box
Big house, little house, cardboard box
Scream if you wanna go faster
Scream if you wanna go faster

The audience falls out the doors into the
bagging area.

# A VAGUE RECOLLECTION OF A TWAT

Ta matey, I appreciate the effort
but it seems you're making leather kecks and fleeces for the desert
and wouldn't water be a better thing to bring
than a leopard-printed bling-adorned effigy of him...
Is that you? Well thanks mate
It's very nice, but now it's late-ish let us stick to Plan A:
trying to make a means of cultivating food while
dismantling the cult of naked nubile prepubescent females
that's infested us it's in us all
So pitifully blind we didn't see the city fall
and turn to sand while the kings wanked each other off
in think tanks with the doors on em double locked
and Ozymandias writ in gold on the gates
The letters now are laying on the lone level plains
and we, survivors in our makeshift cabins
trying to make do beneath a sign that says Shit Happens

Do you remember all the videos?
Do you remember what they sang –
*all them raps?*
You remember which bragger bragged the brashest
before the whole shitstorm collapsed?
The old man said
"Nah soz I don't remember
I really don't remember none of that
Cos all there is a lot of hot wind here
and a vague recollection of a twat..."

Turns out the city was a shabby shambles
Now we're fashioning scabby sandals from bracken and black brambles
Planting cabbages in black cabs with collapsed axles
Making braziers from gas canisters
Re-establishment is gradual
Under the manholes
a clan gathers, living off damp tampons and rank animals
Wasn't long before man emerged as a proper weirdo
Cross your earlobes, there's frogmen in the Trocadero
as trees fill Trafalgar Square toppling Nelson's Column
and jackdaws and pigeons shit in the Tate Modern's
long galleries, there's a family of badgers up in the House of Commons
The cubs are fucking about with trousers on 'em
They're welcome to 'em. Roofs are made to shelter babies
Cockroaches clamber in the Ministry of Health and Safety
so check your daydreams – humanity's a small flame
where old timers reminisce about before it all changed...

Do you remember all the pop tunes
The methylation and the crack?
The woman with the cleavage and the costumes?
Costumes
The man with the bitches in the back?
The old man said
"Nah soz I don't recall it
I really don't remember none of that
Cos all there is is a serpent in the orchard
And a vague recollection of a twat..."

Blam whoops skibadee
Plan's fucked, chuck your apostles
There appears to be a lot of flim-flam stuck in your potholes
And all the MPs have fucked off to the Cotswolds
To gated communities with turrets clogged with pots of gold
Clink Clank / if it weren't tragic it would be funny
Mervyn King died trying to prove that you could eat money
and Downing Street's coming like a set from Escape From LA
On the plus side, now there's no such thing as a debt you're not able to pay
We do die of diseases we thought had faded away
But at least it's better than being shanked on your neighbour's estate
Pros and cons to the apocalypse / the main con
is it's a fair bit tougher to stay alive since the A bomb
The main pro is no radio to feed us bullshit
only a crazy bloke with a soapbox for a pulpit
singing....

*Roll out your dreams and come*
*The end's not far away*
*Chaos redeems us all*
*The truth shall set you free*
*Death is the final call*
*So get up off your knees*
*and celebrate*
*Celebrate...*

# I PLANTED A TIME BEAN

I planted a time bean
It grew to a worm
The worm was a woman
She wriggled and wriggled
and wriggled and turned
Marjorie Time Bean
as long as a night
rolling in shadows
drowning in spirit
scared of the light
Just for the time bean
Tequila for short
She couldn't be bothered
She wriggled and wriggled
She couldn't be caught
Maggie the Worm-Girl
She couldn't be Love
Cos anything given
was never sufficient
was never enough
So look how we finished
Marjorie's gone
Scattered and gone
back in the soil now
back in the garden
dead as a song

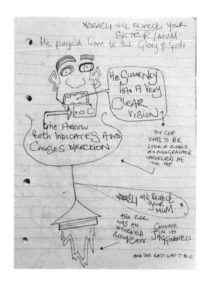

# NICK

I've been in the company of God a lot lately
Spending so much time at his house
I still think his dead son cannot save me
I still feel I need a month out.
Don't get me wrong / churches can be beautiful
in the city when you need a space of calm.
But when it echoes with the dirges of a funeral,
the architecture loses its charm.
And that name on the cover of the programme,
and that face that the name underlines
We used to be friends before the coffin closed, man
We used to share shards of life sometimes.
Now I'm sharing his frozen face with strangers
and I'm standing when I'm told to, like we never did.
In my hand's a tape of '36 Chambers',
the tape he made us which became our teen genesis.

The label still has his writing on it clear
The same he wrote with, passing notes in classroom
The thought of that finds me fighting off a tear –
his tags and his teacher cartoons.
His tag at the time was the word One
with the number written up beside the O.
One would come to mean more than I could know
but at the time, it looked a lot like Lone.
I'm reading too deep / I need to keep it Shotty,
I need to keep it Bong, Hoody, Smile and Kickflip.

I need to shrug my shoulders from the weight of all these bodies;
slip an extra spoon of sugar in like Nick did.
But if I'm reading a little deep, it's not surprising:
I've been in the company of God a lot lately.
So if it's yours to give, God. Give me some time
and I'll make this sacred, before the rot takes me.

# MUDDY AND FUCK

*I've never recorded this one, but I sing it when we need lifting.*

Eh eh / he's a beastie on the beat / so he is
He's a freak and he'll unseat you from your seat / so he will
When you're weepy he'll defeat your many griefs / saying this
*Let's all get muddy and fuck*

AH let's have a threesome in a tipi in a patch of sun
You wang on a CD I'll slip into something masculun
Keep the whisky peaty and the beat fat as a mastodon
*Let's all get muddy and fuck*
Whether you're a beanie or a chap it's on /
Grab a thong
See me as sleazy cos I mash for fun
Your loss / choice is easy: your God's a prude
Mine is catching on
*Let's all get muddy and fuck*

I'm living like a deep-sea Houdini
in a sumptuous garden
You're living like a meat-free panini
in a glove compartment
Who's your judge? Who d'you love?
Who will rub your hard-on?
Let's all get muddy
and fuuuuuuuuuuck

two extraspecial activities made by jesus himself · dancing and bum sex

THINK
I KNOW WHAT
you
MEAN

# CROOK TOOTH
# MISCHIEVOUS

2015-2018

# The Depths / Any Day Now
Dizraeli & The Small Gods (2013)

*Here is a song written by a man still fearful of his own desires, and what their consequences might be. I had had feelings for boys as a boy, and men as a man, and had finally reached the point of coming out as Queer to friends and family (my word, the biggest release of my life. There is so much poison in living with half of you denied and secret.)*

*But I was struggling to find the courage to write the truth of my sexuality in songs, and come out publicly, as an artist. I thought it would somehow be the end of me.*

*Gathering bravery, I wrote a few things that spoke that truth from a sneaky side-angle, in imagery abstract enough to pass unnoticed. 'Minnie The Moocher / Hideously Kinky' is an example of this. And this song, 'The Depths', is another.*

*This is a tangle of voices, this one: the imagined, judging voices of Man in my head; my own judgements of that kind of conventional masculinity; and my own obscure half-confessions and whisperings ("I used to love my cousin... Yetis hunt me, every last one with my father's face..."). I still couldn't quite say it straight (haha).*

*But not long afterwards, the same year this song came out, so did I, onstage at Shambala festival, in front of 4,000 humans. It was like bungee jumping off the fekin moon.*

*Thank you, Amanda, for helping me find the strength to do that. And here's that sideways song.*

# THE DEPTHS

Too unkempt for Soho / Orang u tan in tutu
Smash him back to atoms / Whack him out the tube
The rat'll grab and screw you in a instant
He's insensitive to social imprints
The lad's been mincing
Watch him / he'll have your infants in his pink mittens
Grip your little boys give 'em poisons switch them
Toxify their sex-drives / we don't want the life he's living
We're horrified he's legal and alive and kicking
Kick him / belittle him / reduce him to a smear
His love isn't human / he's Medusa in the mirror
The judgement in the sideways look
Loop of our fear
His love is crooked by the standards of the Great Seer
If you're not the man for women you are eunuch
You are useless to the higher office
You are Devil's music
Cockless / opposite to God, 'course we're scared of you
How dare you do what we don't dare to?

Bellatrix:
*I'd cry but you're too small*
*Your brains are dripping down my wall*
*I don't care*
*You meant nothing to me*
*I don't care*
*You meant nothing to me...*

*I WANT TO SEE THE DEPTHS OH!!*

Then the men come crashing in...

The men are stunted, pig-nosed
Tattoos of women on their torsos
Guns for arms jokes for voices good blokes,
Good blokes / they'll rush the gates
They'll stamp your face into the pavement
if you look close
You're too close
One more inch and you'll be intimate
and intimate is not OK bruv they will string you up
Fisticuffs if you touch what I wish to touch
Vicious efficiency, the skins are buffed / director's cut
Better to show man killing man than man kissing
Man the men'll get you if you dance different
The clan's marching / swinging faggots from a crooked height
Chanting footy anthems as the bullets fly
Me and agony are lookalikes
Cos I been hiding hurt my whole life
Used to love my cousin now I'm shook inside
Shadow in the book of light / I know the dark by name
Yetis hunt me every last one with my father's face
Funny innit / huurh / laugh apart the shame
The punchline is that you're fat or gay
Standard refrain / you half a phrase
You half a man you snake
You evil manifest you castaway
They'll get you....

Bellatrix:
*I'd cry but you're too small*
*Your brains are dripping down my wall*
*I don't care*
*You meant nothing to me*
*I don't care*
*You meant nothing to me...*

## ANY DAY NOW

Any day now
the world will roll out, fold in and over
The iron-sided edifice crumble
The tower tumble
The engine cut
And we can be children again
Any day now
war will die a graceful death out at sea
Meat-wagons burst into flames
Private schools turn to social housing
And we can be children again

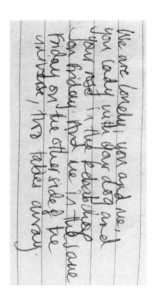

Bellatrix:
*Play your favourite games*
*Play your favourite games...*

While recognising of course that not everybody's childhood was peachy
but still...

The feeling of being able to paint a picture and just
keep still

And Lucifer's still outside in the garden
trying to shout down the morning
But the truth is
none of us here could care
And the walker's still up there on the hill
just trying to shout down the morning
But the truth is
none of us down here could really care

Cos any day now
London will lighten the fuck up
unclench for a minute
put the hammer down
and return the smile
and we can be
children again

Yeah
Any day now
all of us will cut free
Running down Worm Lane
like God's own spies
back to the first place
to the day you learned to whistle

*Play your favourite games*
*Play your favourite games...*

Any day now
She will come round the cliffside
very small to the space in your arms
and it won't seem dangerous
and she will say
'It's alright
We can be children again'

And she will put her arms around you very slow
and make it simple
And Nick will bop down the cliff path lean
and Rob will walk out of the sea with a grin
And the four of you will stand
and watch the waves roll in.

14th August. Isle of Wight

I am standing bollock naked in the forest
unknown things underfoot, flies swerving through the cool air
end of my cock in hand
I'm watching all heaven
break loose

# As We Enter

Dizraeli & DownLow (2015)


Wake up / Dartmoor gathered in storm

My tent tattered and torn

I slept fully dressed / unzip my door

lean in the wind on the moor

Granite and gorse / whipped by a gust of rain

Take me / born child of a hurricane

I am / turn my face upwards

My flesh prey for the buzzards

Lady Death / you're a devil of a sexy bird

I'll get you unless you get me first

Buckle my boots / long as I'm trekking I'm free

Marshes suck at my feet / I'm up to my knees

City kid like me / been a while since I breathed

Suck it all in / derelict tin mines, trees

The footprints I leave

and I've been walking since morning

Now the dark night hits

Never seen stars like this

*switch*

Come with me the country is shapeless

F*ck titties and drugs / cities and wages

Run with me 'til our guts take us

Hungrily to the edge of the cliff / as the day hits

Now then / watch another dawn rise

and sing for the love of your life

I HAVE LITERALLY NO IDEA WHAT I'M DOING.

# Sugarcane Spirit

Dizraeli & Watcha (2016)


*For Ayub Ogada*


Sugarcane spirit in a dark room
Coughing like a cartoon image of a drunk
Bugger-brained / fingering guitar tunes horribly
The harsh truth is that he is done
And he was something like the new hope
Now he's on a chewed rope drinking in the sun
He's eaten nothing for a few days / living out a suitcase
Drinking what has he become?
But he isn't an emotional man
Doesn't cry when he's burying his dad
Doesn't cry when his wife says
You're dead to me / See how high he's carrying his head
So high it could tumble off the back
With the hat still covering the eyes
With the music crumpled up inside
Still mumbling the fun we could've had

And he could've been a rich man
But he settled on a marsh under corrugated iron
Which the wind peels back and slaps round in the background
While he's telling me we're all dying
may as well enjoy hey? Slap, rattle and a burst of rain
Jack'll bring a bottle that'll chase thirst away

For a minute then it rushes back screaming
Bloody-eyed devil, nothing like freedom
Dad died last week from that life
You I give six months 'til you capsize
into the same hole / horribly sad
Still mumbling 'the fun we could've had'

| SUCCESS | FAILURE |
| --- | --- |
| STRENGTH | VULNERABILITY |
| DOING | RESTING |
| BEING KING OF | BEING SUBJECT TO |
| INSPIRING AWE | GIVING A SHIT |
| PENETRATING | BEING PENETRATED |
| ANSWERING | ASKING |
| EDUCATING | GETTING SCHOOLED |
| FIXING THINGS | NEEDING FIXING |
| DESTROYING (incl. myself) | NURTURING (incl. myself) |
| BEING LARGE | BEING SMALL |
| BEING LOVED | BEING LOVING |
| BEING FEARED | FEARING BEING AFRAID |
| HITTING | MISSING |
| HOLDING ON | LETTING GO |
| KILLING (IT) | DEATH. |

15th July

Hundreds of bicycles are in the backyard stacked to a health and safety nightmare, and the girl at the till says "that's got to be the best battered sausage I ever had" while a husky puppy sniffs her flipflops.

There's a beating heart here near Milton Keynes. This woman smiles and has nearly all her hair gone, sponsored by Rockers Ride motorbikes. She sells me tea, though the cafe's supposed to be closed.

Later, further North

Bob hears from the man at the burger van that his friend Tim died last weekend. He collapses for a moment against the side of the van. Ten minutes later, Bob is back in the gazebo, talking shit, pissed on strong beer. A bald man sings bad Aerosmith covers, weirdly lit.

# Eat My Camera - EP
(2016)

## MARVELLOUS

I bought me a mirror
Marvellous
And two new shoes
Marvellous
A Kanyeezus T shirt
Marvellous
Some YouTube views
Marvellous

I bought me a manfriend
Marvellous
Shaped whole out of gold
Marvellous
And he never goes tedious
And he never grows old
Marvellous

I bought me a mirror
Marvellous
And a two-tone suit
Marvellous
A silver chinchilla
Marvellous

And a secret side-boob...
Marvellous

I bought me a mirror
And a thoroughborn hound
A merry-go-round and around in Ibiza
Forever go round

I bought me a brick of a house in LONDON
Well / a promise of a brick
The grandkiddy of my grandkiddy's grandkiddy
Will still pay for it
Marvellous

But I bought me a mirror
Marvellous
& cellophane wing
So really give a frig what you telling me mister
I can do anything
Anything
Anything...

Jim got stabbed for a packet of Rizla
John got shot for a packet of seeds
Cindy slipped through a crack in the picture
Didn't see the crows sat in the trees
But it's easy when you know
How the money runs...
Said it's easy when you know
How the money runs...

# EAT MY CAMERA

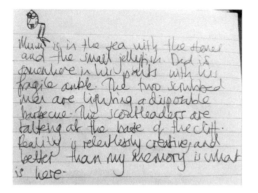

I am spangled off the trees sir
Literally the trees sir
I'm powered off the eggs of
Easter
Peace love and the salt of the
sea sir
And I'm done with the role of
the preacher
I see birds swing on the wind from all angles
The sap surging from all angles
Root-hairs grab at your ankles
The plan is
Run along a coast path nude
With your own track playing in your belly on loop
and your cranium full of the fruits of the soil
Very enjoyable
Gimme a ding when you're done with it
There's a plan B that is just as sick
Last one to the sea is a crusty dick
We'll swim through the lens to the substance

*Rocks split / fracture / fragments cast as black birds*
*cast on the wind's howl*
*They'll eat my camera*
*Breezeblock gasworks*
*Madman wracked with cancer*
*Starving starling come and*
*eat my camera*

*And on and on the river rolls*
*on and on the river rolls*

Oh shit what a fabulous face you own
I can think of a place to go
Where the wind blows blue through the windows
and the smoke can erase you slow
That's it Hun
the dust settles
You're where the drunk kids come to chuck pebbles
Green and it's grey and it's full of birdshit
Cos the birds come here to die
Or procreate I don't know
the roof here is full of holes
There's a mattress and a cracked bowl
and a smell of piss warm and old
I put flowers in the corner for ya
Well not flowers exactly
But the thought of flowers, count them
There's as many as there possibly can be
Pluck some you're the Queen of Hackney
You look beautiful in brown
Just as pretty as the day you drowned
Come occupy my substance
Come occupy my substance
Come occupy my substance
Come occupy my substance

*Rocks split / fracture / fragments cast as black birds*
*cast on the wind's howl*
*They'll eat my camera*

*Breezeblock gasworks*
*Madman wracked with cancer*
*Starving starling come and*
*eat my camera*

*And on and on the river rolls*
*And on and on the river rolls*
*And on and on the river rolls*
*And on and on the river rolls*

So tell me what counts as church
This whole frigging county's church
The furze and the rocks and the birds
Carry candles
Watch your words

*So tell me what counts as church*
*This whole frigging county's church*
*The furze and the rocks and the birds*
*Carry candles*
*Watch your words*

*Tell me what counts as church*
*This whole frigging county's church*
*The furze and the rocks and the birds*
*Carry candles.*

# ARIANE

Wait a minute have we got no time for love?
The flame was vivid but it's stopped now wind it up
Cos you seen me striding through your future with that father strength /
Arnie style
Holding your home and your heart and your ornaments
But that's not me see
Dragging a caravan, my crotch locked just for you
Polishing tea sets / he said / she said in dusty rooms
I must keep breathing
Surely my freedom was what you were attracted to... Yeah?
The love of air
The bird'll fade shut away in that tupperware

It goes
*Ariane, Ariane, Ariane*
*You have changed since the summer...*

And I'm not saying your demands weren't standard ones
Perfectly flipping standard
And maybe I'm a punk fool who can't handle luck
You are a catch and stuff
I know
My aunt loved you and my brother thought you were sound
Real sound...
It's gonna be harsh when Christmas rolls around
It's November and I'm thinking of your hips 'til I'm hardly there
My mother says she misses you and that's hard to bear

And if I'm honest I regret being what I am
I could wither and die
I'd die happy if my love you would just reply...

It goes
*Ariane, Ariane, Ariane*
*You have changed since the summer...*


## COOL & CALM


*A river runs through here*
*once in a year*
*Everybody stay cool and calm*
*Cos up at the border*
*a teen boy's got a gun*
*Everyone stay cool and calm*
*Down past the Dead Sea*
*there are bodies stretched out in the sun*
*Stay cool and calm*
*I'm on a bus full of soldiers*
*They're playing slapsies down the front*
*Stay cool and calm...*

Every brick is full of legend
Pilgrims file down the narrow lanes
like a long line of silly little questions
looking for a miracle ascension
Fences hold 'em back

Shuffle footed sheep, branded shoulder bags
This a holy land / you can tell it from the barbed wire
Roped off relics / adolescent men in car tyre
Roadblocks / and the wall, the Wall.
That turns me to a flabbergasted fool
in an avalanche of stories
too heinous to believe
I see my father dragged out and beaten in the street
I see my cousin screaming down the barrel of a tank's gun
The tanned young soldier who is hideously handsome
Looking blank back at him / overspilling with the times
Nineteen with a military mind
wearing billabong and Calvin Klein
at the barracks with his child friends
He's loving and he's civil and he's kind
He's loving and he's civil and the pulls the trigger in a blind terror
and my cousin's blown into never-never
with brains spattered over the divide as we're watching
Tell us then. What are our options?

*A river runs through here*
*once in a year*
*Everybody stay cool and calm*
*Cos up at the border*
*everyone has got a gun*
*Stay cool and calm*
*Down past the Red Sea*
*they are laying bodies out in the sun*
*Stay cool and calm*
*I'm in a room full of soldiers*
*They're playing truth or dare down the front*
*Stay cool and calm...*

Calais. Blog. 5th December

It's a mild, windless evening in the so-called Jungle, and there's a soft stink of urine and burning plastic. We pick our way around puddles and potholes, finding a path among the endless guyropes, patched-together tents and shacks towards Omar's place. In the camp I have my bearings less than half the time, and the landscape changes so fast that even then I'm fumbling. The great raised eyebrow which arches over the camp's entrance is the flyover which takes trucks and cars to the ferry port nearby, and the gap beneath it always seems to fix your gaze. French riot police, the CRS, swarm the eyebrow in their mock-sinister combat getup, their shoulder pads and hinges looking like Stormtroopers vs. Ninja Turtles. They are watching for trouble and waiting for nightfall, when a number of the people from the camp will go to The Chance (as Omar calls it with typical poetic skill) – the hiding, running, climbing, leaping ritual in which they try to get themselves aboard a lorry or train bound for the UK. The great majority of them will fail; many will be beaten by the Storm Turtles. Anecdotes of being hit with batons and verbally abused are two a penny when you talk with people here. In the CRS, all the hatred and intolerance that bubbles below the surface of our Civilisation finds its expression, and they stand proud and swing hard with the honour.

We wave to people as we pass: Darla has spent months here and knows pretty much everyone. She gives me snatches of their stories as we go: that woman arrived from Cameroon three days ago penniless, shoes destroyed by walking, and spent two days in the camp without eating anything, not speaking English and not knowing where to find food; that shy fifteen-year-old boy arrived from Iraq on his own and has no relatives or friends here; that man is the father of the small boy he's with – the boy has a throat condition which is getting worse by the day, and his dad is desperate to leave the camp and find somewhere warm for his son to sleep. We stop often to talk to people, and greet others in passing – a group of men sitting round an acrid fire; a man trying to split wood with a hammer. Darla reminds me that as well as there being woefully inadequate resources here to make homes, a lot of the people come from cities where they worked office jobs or in retail – they have as much grasp of carpentry as I do (very little); most have never even put up a tent before and have to be shown how when they arrive at the 'Jungle'. Being here was never part of anyone's plan.

We have a brief conversation with Ahmed from Syria, who fled airstrikes and Isis brutality in his hometown, crossed the sea from Turkey to Greece in a dinghy with 62 other people in it, was attacked by the Greek special forces and had to swim the last stretch to Lesvos, was smuggled through Serbia by a Mafia man he paid 1500 euros for the privilege, almost suffocated in the back of a flour tanker and now has spent 43 days in the camp. If anyone has a legitimate claim to a breather and a comfortable bed, it's Ahmed: but now he must find the energy and cunning to stow away on a lorry or a moving train with Swarm Turtles chasing, and stay hidden until England. He's already been discovered and sent back to the camp twice doing this.

We move on, past the Jungle Books library, past the Eritrean church in its weird semi-permanence (corrugated iron with a plywood walled enclosure; crucifix on the roof), past the Theatre geodome where we spent all day doing workshops and speaking Music (the one common language in the camp), past a barrel in which someone's burning a sleeping bag, which is fed in gradually like a lolling tongue retracting, black smoke crawling upwards into the still air; and now into the Sudanese area. The Sudanese area is tidier and better-built than much of the rest of the camp; many of the people here from Sudan, for whatever reason, arrive with enough practical skills to construct passable shacks.

Across the big puddle, over the pothole and we're there – Omar's place. It's a tiny, sturdy shack which he built himself from donated wood and tarp; smaller than a garden shed. Omar comes to the door smiling: "you are most welcome", and we're gestured inside. There's a candle burning, and just about space for a small camp bed, two rickety chairs and a butane stove. There are fifteen different varieties of beans in tins on a shelf, and rice and pulses in a box below. Everything is impeccably organised. Omar's friend Mohammed is chopping onions into a frying pan, and greets us warmly too. Omar and Mohammed travelled from the Sudan together – they're old friends. Unlike Omar, Mohammed's English is minimal, but he has a gentle, gangly presence that I feel immediately at ease in: one of those people whose company slows me down and stops me worrying. He shows me the palm of his hand which is bisected by a vicious scar. It's not an injury he got in Darfur, the civil war he escaped from, but a wound inflicted two months ago by the white fences of Calais. The sight of it brings tears to my eyes. The whole existence of the camp is a sad, stinking indictment of the state of the world, but something about Mohammed breaks my heart especially. I see my mate Dave in him, another gentle, loping human. Tall soft Dave, who was always yelled at by the P.E. teacher for dropping the ball, and who was always the one I went to if I needed to talk something through. Dave, Mohammed. Some people are just not meant for running, hiding, climbing. Mohammed shouldn't be here. He should be somewhere safe and warm, telling stories and reaching with long arms and making the vibes excellent. Fucksake. No-one should be here.

The onions begin to sizzle in a puddle of oil, and the at-home smell of that fills the darkness. Darla and Omar are sitting on the camp-bed talking about a poem that Omar wrote, which he's showing her on his phone. Omar has begun to write his poetry in English since arriving at the camp, and at the theatre dome earlier he showed me a couple of pieces. They were properly good; lean observations of camp life written with a freshness and jumble that I often love in writers who don't come from English. Darla says this poem, though, is her favourite of his. She asks if he'd show it to me – he shrinks away and is reluctant. Omar is thoughtful and very soft-spoken, not a performer at all, and today is particularly quiet. He apologises: "I am not in a good mood. I'm sorry". He tells us that today he cycled into Calais to get something from the shops there. The police stopped him and asked "do you speak French?" He said No. "Do you speak English?" He said no; sometimes it's better to be inaccessible. "Do you speak Arabic?" He nodded, and they stabbed the tyres of his bike with a screwdriver.

"Why would someone do that?" He doesn't understand. "I was just walking, you know, in the town, not even near the trains..."

We offer some condolences, some useless apologies and indignation, and then fall silent. We often are struck dumb like this, in the camp. In the grand scheme of injustice this incident is minor, but the truths it represents are so huge and horrible, at times it seems impossible to do anything but shake our heads: this hierarchy of language and culture that you must be on the right rung of to be allowed through; the violence of the act itself; the vulnerability of someone in a situation where the men at the last line of defence are the perpetrators of the very abuse against which they should defend you. Worst of all, as if the terrors of Darfur from which Omar has fled were not enough, that he should be punished here, now, for trying to escape those terrors. 'How dare you want a life as safe as ours?', the policemen say, 'how dare you bring your difference to our town?'...

A whoosh of steam goes up. Mohammed turns to us and grins, the emptied tin of beans in his hand. Omar goes to the plastic box and picks out salt and spices, and shakes showers of both into the pan. We all stare into the stew, watching it become a rich swamp of goodness, smelling the horn-grabbing smells it's sending up, brains alive with the impossible facts of the Camp, mouths watering. Before long it's ready, but only me and Darla are served -

"Omar, Mohammed, are you not eating?" No, no – "it is for you", they say, "we have already eaten"... All of this, for us. It's as powerful, warm and delicious as it smelled and we eat heartily while Mohammed smiles into his phone and plays Sudanese music on YouTube – women singing passionate duets, stately men in armchairs playing violins, and always a big chorus of singers joined together for the refrain. We eat while Omar sits back on the camp bed, his face unreadable.

After we finish, he hands me his phone and I read the poem on it: it is full of ghosts and wide open places, and it's addressed to someone who is drowning. It is horribly beautiful. After the third time reading it I look up.

"It is for my best friend", Omar answers quietly, "he died crossing with me to Europe".

That silence again.

There is such a lot to do.

# MORNING LIGHT

*Running in the morning light*
*Trying to catch a falling tide*
*Running in the morning light*
*Pressure out the window*
*Running in the morning light*
*Trying to catch a seed of time*
*Running in the morning light*
*Pressure...*

Look - I'm not particularly deadly
Though I carry arms I'm not afraid to use
Being I'm a doer, I be doing
Balls deep, clambering the cliffs in a scruffy set of shoes.
So don't invite me to your poncy little dinner
Though I am pretty handy with your codes
Stick me in the cellar with the swingers
They are more my scene / Come strip me of my clothes...
Cos I can hold a pose for minutes, even hours
But eventually something sours
Something flings itself around in me
Yelling 'Now it's time to frigging wriggle out your trousers
pulling people out their pouches'
Running in the morning light
The marshland couldn't give a frig for me
It is a space out of history
Bury my visage in its mudholes
And when the day rises I have struck gold...

Geese fly in celebration / That's my church
I prefer the wind over any kind of audience
When I chat my words I launch my soul
People say there's madness in the heat of my performance.
Maybe so. Maybe there'll be sorrow on my deathstone
Maybe I'll be geriatric nutter bombing Tesco.
At least I'll have been honest from the get-go
I'm honestly the opposite of London

*Running in the morning light*
*Trying to catch a falling tide*
*Running in the morning light*
*Pressure out the window*
*Running in the morning light*
*Trying to catch a seed of time*
*Running in the morning light*
*Pressure...*


Daddy was a preacher man
He spoke the Holy Ghost at peace protests
We reclaimed the streets together
Sweet Moses part the asphalt
Tell it like a town crier / Light the fuse
They will never televise the news
All he taught me / He born in 1940s
Truths that he had to fight to find
Me born in Thatcherite decline
Same appetite for life
I learnt sanity from Catcher In The Rye

Now the stamina is mine / The wild animus
The caravan standing in the vines
The grizzly bear is mine / The piston and the steam
Forever back in Bristol in my dreams
And the world is often ending in them
And that is often cause for joy.
I'm back in adolescence in a wall of noise
Banging a snare drum / clocking how they murder us slow
Dad, come: we've got further to go...

*Running in the morning light*
*Trying to catch a falling tide*
*Running in the morning light*
*Pressure out the window*
*Running in the morning light*
*Trying to catch a seed of time*
*Running in the morning light*
*Pressure...*

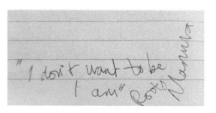

## DONA DIAZ

*I've got a reason to live*
*She's called Dona Diaz*
*She's got a rolling stride*
*And she waddles when she runs*
*But that's alright*

*I met her in a house of thorns*
*She told me she'd never be mine*
*Oh I was her slave for a day*
*But then she fell into my arms*
*And that's alright*

*She took me to a cave by the sea*
*She showed me her strange insides*
*Ah she's nasty and she's brave and she's free*
*And she grinds her teeth all night*
*But that's alright*

*Ah my Maria*
*Tie me up*
*My blue flame*
*Tie me up*
*My Boadicea*
*Tie me up*
*You Holy War*
*When you wed me*
*I will take your name*
*And wave it like a neon sword*

*I've got a reason to live*
*She's called Dona Diaz*
*She's got a rolling stride*
*And she waddles when she runs*
*But that's alright...*

BEMUSER TRY ANGLE

---

Green Lanes. 24th May

It's hard keeping Timothy out of the fuckin monologue right now. I'm
feeling small and unmusical and not good. A battle swinging back and
forth in my head, general lack of love and a feeling of fading.

HOld

it

together.

# Leroy Merlin - EP
Dizraeli & DownLow w/ Nathan Feddo (2017)


## JOHN THE BAPTIST


He has the powers of the winds in him
It's impossible to stand still
Thoughts bustle like an anthill colony
The man's ill / buzzing like a superthrust Excalibur
Live from the uterus of planet earth
Mama come and tie him down
You were right about the quiet people
You have to watch em they are riot shields
Fire guards / which conceal lion hearts
Megawatts the wire charged
Stretched across a chasm that is
Too much / Somebody make him normal
His brain is overspacious
Clothes draped over a naked mortal
Naked mole-rat / Look – he struck a weird pose
Shaking like a leaf in autumn / Plucks his earlobes
And mutters something most unsettling
It's hard enough holding our shit together knowing vast-
ness is a part of us
Without the evidence presented to us in a human form
His eyes are two balls of hunger grabbing at a fuschia
dawn
Dressed in flamboyant trousers

Tootling a flugelhorn
Dancing at the crux of all that matters
Arms cruciform
Fool up in the eunuch's court / The man's too damn alive
Too unsanitized / Tie him down

*aaaaaaaaaaaaaaaaaaaaaaaaaaaaaaaah*

I've got visions in my head bruv
Or is it pigeons in my head?
Whatever it is
There isn't any let up
Flapping and they're feverish
Carry me back home, flagstones
I'm carrying a flagon fulla Jesus
Or is it flagon fulla sheep piss

Don't know but I ain't emptying my catheter in secret
Stokes Croft's my living room
I'm married to the street / she's a cheap bitch
But I int enamoured of these eejits
prancing through my lounge
You see their privilege / They carry it around
However ragged are their jeanses
Their eyes are sitting comfortable
So why they criticise the style of life I'm living fuck em all
I'll fight em if they come to call
That's real talk / I'll steel claw em / That's provided I can still walk
I spill morphine out my ears / I'm brimming over breezing
In a t-shirt / Though it's Minnesota freezing
There's a reason I am John the Baptist
Or is it John the Batshit

Crazy as a clod of cabbage me
Lost to madness
Or is it majesty that causes starlight to blur?
Tonight'll be my last night on earth
I can feel it
I can feel it
I can feel it
I can feel it
I can feel it
I can feel it

coming

# DYLAN THOMAS

Raggedy android / back on the bill
Fresh born from a crack in the hill
and still striving
I wear my body like a tangerine peel
So don't wave your flag at me / chill
I'm near skyborn
Rather Rimbaud than Rambo
I'm on a ramble
Ram's skull up in my satchel
Pull up in a banger real casual
Pull on my mackintosh
Last strip of asphalt
before the black moors
Killer dog boglins
Cash rules nothing round here
This is Bodmin
So I'm done ticking boxes
Sick of jogging
treadmills
Fish abundant here / stick a rod in
Moon kotch / Activate your shoebox brain
There's a dragon in your boombox the tune got strange
Misplace marbles lose plots mate
There's a dragon in your boombox the tune got strange
It's a *unghh....*

I lost my welly in the marshes....

*Before I saw her die*
*I didn't know what it was to be alive...*

The mist's lifted / the eye narrows for the extra light
A festival of colour bless the sight
Garden / A garbled canister of words
and he stands among the fir trees / a panoply of urges
The kid's a nervous twitch / Rebirth's a difficult procedure
The earth's his / that twiddles his receivers
A grizzly creature comes along to sniff him
and passes / he's no different than thunder from a distance
truth of the world / watching its own breath
Off of the time train / not conscious of progress
He tightens his mind to a silvery bullet / like that of a hawk owl
Casts it into the gullet of a raggedy dormouse
and rides it into the rushes with its jittery steps
Never more than a millisecond from death
Shivering flesh capsule / knows it is food for a predator's gut
Suddenly stock still / he presses his belly to mud
While a creature stinking of off milk looms like a
ogre past him on the path / it's a human hiker
Huge clumper / lump of deformity
Hideous hunk of bones, skin and enormous teeth
How can an animal of that size stay upright
without folding into its own axis or capsizing?
It's a miracle of willpower he thinks / fuck that
And fades into the marsh as a mist
Never to come back

*Before I saw her die*
*I didn't know what it was to be alive...*

2nd Dec

From a brushed hand across the table to a street snog,
to a leg on leg in the dressing room to a snatched hour
in her bedroom smelling of incense, living the life
before dying.

Inching towards the truth

## HAVE A RUM

*And I just hope you're somewhere*
*good right now*
*If I was there I'd make it better*
*But as you have seen fit to cut me out*
*I suppose I'll have a rum*

*Ma nana*
*Tu vas te faire mal comme ca*
*Tu vas te faire mal comme ca*
*Ma nana*
*Tu vas te faire mal comme ca*
*Tu vas te faire mal comme ca*

I wish you bright yellow memories
A warm centre and a head for humans
An eye for splendour and a sense of movement
Cash enough you're not swinging from a chewed length of shoestring
Enough to get the train and strength of brain to drink the views in
Presence in your space in such ways
Your day is unstained by making up ways
to frame it as a status update
I wish you knowledge of your own needs
and words to speak 'em
Wish you to be home free / to be never lonely
To wake up in a room that's full of air and sun
For somebody who gets your oddness to be there to hug
you like you want them to / including room for honest truth
Someone you can read Dylan Thomas to
And they will never cock a snook or say Very Nice Dear
when you tell 'em heaven's right here
Look look / the view's amazing / if you ignore the smell of piss / the highest
kings are not living as well as this
And you squeeze the elegance from charity shop shoes
and pride from the tenner they cost you
Nothing stretches further / than your eye for bargains
Though in another life you're made for first class compartments / you're an
empress / I wish you feta cheese, bread and port / and to be freed from money
worry now and ever more / I wish you to be high as heaven / fortyseventh
floor / with fizzy wine and all your friends in red feathers and leather drawers
/ You're better than me / I wish you self-love to know that / you built a marvel
off your own back / I wish you good rum, a hammock / warm breeze / but
more than all these / I wish you'd call me.

*And I just hope you're somewhere good right now*
*If I was there I'd make it better*
*But as you have seen fit to cut me out*
*I suppose I'll have a rum*

*And all I wrote and all I said was love*
*I'm pretty sure she got that letter*
*And so she knows I know I fucked this up*
*I suppose I'll have a rum*

*Ma nana*
*Tu vas te faire mal comme ca*
*Tu vas te faire mal comme ca*

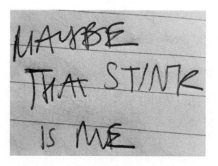

# Leroy Merlin - The Mixtape
(2017)

## INTRO

*Fling it out sir / Fling it out*
*Give 'em something to reach for*
*Love all the people*
*Clutching their beers and their men and women*
*Lining the seashores*
*Looking out*
*Tell us what it is they see*
*Whatever it may be they see, look*
*They see themselves*
*The whole picture's a reflection of their innards*
*Sinners see sinners / Swingers see sex*
*Victim sees viciousness*
Standard / So why'm I meddling with language?
Simple – trying to give them all mantras to unify / It's tough
Some of them would sooner die than love
But at 12.35 on a Wednesday it's worth it
Every dirtminded freakoid here's perfect
I move among 'em with a grin stay artist
Moonfaced / waving as the train passes
I move slow seeing things stay searching
B boy / Freakoid / Leroy Merlin

26th Oct

Talking with Nick H about Buddhist sand pictures, where every stage of the creation is done in the spirit of impermanence, with dedication and painstaking thoroughness, total mindfulness, and then the image is lost to time...

There is God in everything all the time. Spoon, tree, power station, bicycle.

# BATA BOY

*I'll be your crook tooth mischievous*
*I'll be that fruit you find*
*I'll be your good book's wickedness*
*I'll be your hot dark mind*
*I'll be your pride bent over*
*I'll be your good God's blame*
*I'll be your moon-eyed monster*
*I'll be your father's shame...*

Boy in a playground, boy in a scrum
Boy with a deep secret
Boy with a hard face
Boy with a lust
Keeps that hidden
Boy with a heartache, boy with a crush
Boy with a twist
Boy with a classmate, boy that he loves
Boy makes fist
Boys are a bastard, Boys are a jail
boys are a dick
Boy can it be nasty to be born male
Boys are a click
Click of the ratchet, Click of the glock
Click of the phone
Click of the catches
Click of the lock
Now click they're alone

Boy with a boy now
Boy with a kiss
Boy with a squeeze
Boys keep noise down
Boys in bliss
Boys in the heat
Boys'll be boys though. Ten boys burst in
Slaps and yells
Boy you're a homo
Boys boys hurt him
Don't check yourselves.

He said
but the world's all cool for the queers now
Now Cameron's passed his bill
I said
you ever held hands with a man on a high street
Felt how that feels?
You ever felt fear of attack? Been slapped cos of what you are?
Been shunned cos of what you are
Been told you're disgusting for what you are?
I have and the world ain't London
My sun and the world ain't free
I step with a humpback knowing that the
Boys with the shotgun brains hate me
We are one short step from the 80s
One election from Trump
Senegal to Iraq to Haiti
Somerset where they call queers scum
And I got a slap for the asshole
Who's threatened by the way we love

One slap for the preacher man boy idiot
Spreading his shame on us
I got a mate whose Dad disowned him
I got a mate whose mum won't speak
I got a mate who says that's gay and he means
That's wack and he means that's weak
Them words put bats in the belfry
Put boys in a twisted shape
Watch close how the rot grows
Plant hate in the brain and the kid decays
Self hate be the fruit of bigotry
Hell waits with a winking eye
Your jokes will abuse our dignity
Pure shit from a stinking mind
And fuck you Tony Perkins
I be that flood you foretold
And love to Amir Ashour
Let me know if you need support
And we'll be that rude truth spoken
We'll be that crowd stood strong
We'll be that vigil unbroken
We'll be that protest song
We'll be that massed proud people
We'll be that flame still lit
We'll be that hand
that hold
that family
that air,
that fist

# PAINT FLOWERS

i said. That's a pretty masquerade
A vivid little grimace for the tit for tat parade
Sorry bruv, I didn't catch your name
I was on my back listening to the pitter pat of rain
Listen / it's impossible how slow
and silent everything operates / cacophony of growth
And the soil has a proper sweet cologne
Isn't often you enjoy it / Isn't often we're alone
And is it shocking? / Is it shocking you to know
that when nobody is watching you're a cockle you're a stone
you're a mollusc you're a fragment of a fossil of a bone
of a prehistoric possum with a telescopic toe
What I mean is the truth couldn't give a turd
for the cleanness of your creps or the leanness of your beanie
or the heinous little set of codes weaving through your words
There's no excuse for cliché you're jesus you are sea-deep

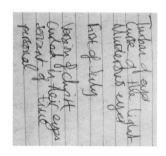

*original / turn your brain outwards*
*Nobody's trodden in the same trousers*
*The force / force formidable*
*the taste sours*
*but you / face the wall and paint flowers / Paint flowers /*
*Stained glass*
*window pane / clownish*
*saints dance in the late hours*
*it's all, all original / you have insane powers*
*kick the wall down and paint flowers*
*Paint flowers*

Come pulverise the wall and paint rockets in the air
Or are u busy putting toxins in your hair
Madam? wrapped in nylon tights and typing til the lights gone
While I'm off to wig out under pylons with my gods
Who are well adept at pointing out the glories
Interpreting silhouettes and boisterously saucy
Sorcery blatant in the crosshatching of cabling
Against the grinning moon that saves her last love for the vagrants dem
I'm a vagrant I'm a vagrant ooh
I blacked out as housecat and came to as sabretooth
Able to penetrate your noggin with a pair of punctures
Til your ability to square logic barely functions
Welcome to underland where you can
Wear your ugly pants without some bureaucrat tugging your bungee down
I'm a bungee jumper / I'm a swordfish in some funky swimwear
peddling jugs of summer on the tundra
I swim with sunk wrecks / and suckle sailors on their sun decks
and wrestle flame-headed goblins and forbidden subjects
Son you a sorry sight / blinded in the fog of time
Slapping stickers on your eyelids / Fighting with your pocket knife
Try this'll have you undressing boggle-eyed and lopsided
Writhing under copper skies / God-minded

*You're original / turn your brain outwards*
*Nobody's trodden in the same trousers*
*The force / force formidable*
*the taste sours*
*but you / face the wall and paint flowers*
*Paint flowers / Stained glass*
*window pane clownish*

*saints dance in the late hours*
*it's all, all original / you have insane powers*
*kick the wall down and paint flowers*
*Paint flowers*

## JUST LIKE YOU

Crimson / velvet / they are lovely / the lips love me
I am drinking melted honey / watch the flesh become me
London / running noisy rings around the north circ
The noise far far out at the edges looking awkward
Yah yah city bustle / You have no space here
Face to face with her / her gaze clear

It could erase me if I let it / set it in amber
Let it spread its light to the wretched of the damp earth
Then bring it / back to Hackney / to this specific back street
So I can stand and kiss it in this manner exactly
Pretty perfect / Kitty work it
Our mouths are a pair of O's / like that famous civil servant
Strong bond / pulses pulsing like a manic pair of Tom Toms
Gilded with a gold emulsion
Pretty kitsch / but that's the old emotion
Grabbing at our crotches holding us
We grabbed it back and dove in / man it's potent

*The prospect of sex looming*
*with a human*
*with a body this warm -*
*the fruit blooming*
*Too right I'm guided by it*
*A truth proven*
*but fucking is a fucking riot / just fuckin lush*
*and I'm dying just like you*
*I'm dying just like you...*

Eh eh she's a rotten lovely
Come we run away, become free
The valley air looking comfy
and it's here for us / Let's get nude in it.
Give it our skin - skin on skin / A fruit fillet
for the hungry eye / eh Lullaby
Put your arms around / rest your head on me
I've come alive

The whole paddock sees it
We're in the shadow of the tree
I'm gulping huge hoops of air
She is shallow breathing
Eyes shut / glitter on her cheek
I look up / The leaves titter on at me
and why not / We are silly creatures with our thrust urges
But she is blooming in the high flush of perfect
I saw it in her as she leaned across the barrier
She is a winner with a goddess as her avatar
And now we're six hours richer in the daylight
I swear blind - if she kisses me I'll take flight

*It's the prospect of sex looming / with a human*
*with a body this warm / the fruit blooming*
*Too right I'm guided by it / A truth proven*
*but fucking is a fucking riot / just fuckin lush*
*and I'm dying just like you*
*I'm dying just like you*

*And it's up to us / We've been up for days*
*We are reprobates / We're runaways*
*Becoming strange in the summer dust / Gone astray*
*Love we are vagrants we are runaways*
*It's up to us / We been up for days*
*We are reprobates / We're runaways*
*Becoming strange in the summer dust*
*Gone astray / Love we are vagrants we are runaways*
*Love......... love*

I'm in a port town at the end of the world
I'm in a loft room at the end of the world
I'm in a cold field at the end of the world
I'm smelling your skin at the end of the world
I'm on a UK tour at the end of the world
I'm picking apricots at the end of the world
I'm kissing Omar at the end of the world

# YOU TALK ABOUT MONEY

*In memory of Passing Clouds*

See me on a couch with a beer and a blown mind laughing
The Clouds – where you do not see time passing
The Clouds – where you have the whole known Dalston
All colours all backgrounds
The Clouds holds them
Holds us
White shirts. High rollers. Glitter imps smothered in gold dust
Buffalo soldiers
Here's where we go home when we go out
While the scary-go-round goes round
Outside the whole town's
gone screwy
What do we do we come here
where the floor's solid as a pronoun
Even as it bounces to the fresh grown sounds
of the next generation in a hoe-down
Knees up, splinter-toed. We're a little broke
We're the little blokes
Humans / never close to the middle road
We are out here / we're the makers
We are Donny Hathaway / we are Miles Davis
We are bad sleepers / good neighbours / stepping razors
Giants in our small damp spaces
While you walk around like bank statements

We talk about midnight / you talk about money
We talk about food / you talk about money
We talk about future / you talk about money
You talk about money / you talk about money
We talk about roots / you talk about money
We talk about ways out / you talk about money
We talk about children / you talk about money
You talk about money / you talk about money

Now money takes our town and paints it grey
And they're playing Bob Dylan in the Starbucks
And they're playing Joni singing we are stardust
And then it's don't know what you got til it's
Shuttered up and dog-patrolled
They take out Cable
They take out Troubadour
They take Astoria
They take out Turnmills
They take out Hammersmith Palais
They take out Marquee
They take out Mean Fiddler
The Twelve Bar
The Coronet
They take our Silver Bullet
They take our Silver Bullet
They take our Fabric
They take our Fabric
So scrub out Bob Dylan
Scrub out the Rolling Stones
Scrub the Beatles out
Scrub out Marvin Gaye

Scrub out Stevie Wonder
Scrub out Nina
Scrub the Who out
Scrub out Amy Winehouse
Scrub out Otis Redding
Scrub out Jimi
Scrub out Miles
Scrub out Donnie
Scrub out James
And paint it all grey
And talk about money

But we talk about music / you talk about money
We talk about sanity / you talk about money
We talk about people / you talk about money
We talk about trust / you talk about money
We talk about home / you talk about money
We talk about home / you talk about money
We talk about home / you talk about money
you talk about money
you talk about money
you talk about money

I'm most effectual when I remember to laugh. This is a great gasping, sobbing farce of a world we've woven ourselves into.

# COMING HOME

2018-2022

# MY BROTHER CAN'T
# HELP HIMSELF (2017)

My brother can't help himself
My brother can't help himself
He looks at                    tits
My brother's all on my back
All up in my books and vids
That crook eyed          dick
Can't help himself

My brother can't talk at all
He dosey doe's
He makes your tears to mockery
Cos he can't cope with those
Ah bro my bro
My brother rock fort
All of the way to the core
Ox                          boar
Billygoat bear
No buddy don't go there

    Nor there
        nor there
    Pretty much go nowhere
    My brother's all shooken and
    scared
        You'd never know though
        Ah bro my bro

You are one lonely hero
Stony mofo. Only one road here
My bony old bro
You roam it alone
Nobody there but he
Beasts in the dark ugly
        Beasts in the dark!

    Don't get his goat
    He will get his boys
    He will get his gun
    Don't get him wrong
    If you get his goat
    My brother goes


blank.

my brother can't think.
my brother can't think.
don't ask questions of him
my brother can't think Party time!
My brother does just the one sniff
Then another then another one
Then another then another then
        another one
My brother's munted
Just for fun
My brother's quite mardy

My brother's quite gone
My brother's quite ill
My brother's quite ill
My brother might

.

him

self

My brother can't help himself
My brother can't help himself
My brother can't help himself

28th Oct

I'm not gonna apologise. I'm just gonna do this. I want
to make true noise. Say the shit that needs saying.

# The Unmaster
(2019)

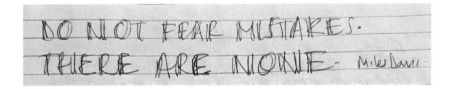

I'M A WAVE (PART ONE)

*| atmos: kebab shop ventilation unit, Green Lanes |*

*I'm a wave I'm a wave my darling*
*I arise I arise I'm done*
*All love to the deep beneath me*
*All love to whoever shall come...*

# MADNESS

There's a madness in the world today
A billion fragments in a tidal wave
The wave crashes up the old Green Lanes
And everybody's eyes are barmy

Must hurry there's a frantic rush
Up in the cafes and the cancer bus
In seven minutes we turn back to dust
And everybody's eyes are barmy

Eyes are barmy and our backs are sprained
Muscles spasming in nasty ways
Faces glisten like we're cast in clay
Ah look at everybody's eyes

None of these signifiers answers us
Professor Sanake and Captain Crush
Lady Ladbrokes and the Abacus
Everybody's eyes are barmy

And it's a crash it's an emergency
It paints a long and livid purple scream
All up the turnpike to Bounders' Green
ah look at everybody's eyes

A machine collapses at the hospital
A stack of polystyrene boxes falls
And out the panic room a monster crawls
Everybody's eyes are sick

So stop your scribbling and stay your pen
They're putting needles in the rain again
A planet governed by insane young men
And everybody's eyes are barmy...

*Aaaaaoooooooooohhhhhhhh...*
*It's madness*

*Just too much it's too*
*Much*
*It's much too much it's too*
*Much*
*It's just too much it's too*
*Much*
*It's much too much it's too...*

## THE WORLD TILTS SIDEWAYS

Paris is in flames. London is in flames

The world tilts sideways.

A man staggers at junkie speed up the pavement, his
eyes long-term unhappy. He violently sticks his hand
into the money slot of the parking meter, and vanishes.

Tell me that you love me.

# KETAMINE HONEY

She is trapped in a constant mania
I am trapped in a small dark room
Hearing her laugh through the bricks and paintwork
Hearing her laugh like a warped cartoon
She is pretty but her eyes are spider eyes
Her tongue is an amphetamine lizard
The house fills with a fucked up firelight
When she comes round everything fizzes
And perhaps they are watching videos
Perhaps screwing it is hard to tell
Whatever doing the noise is hideous
Godzilla versus Gargamel
But she is trapped and I see her fluttering
She's desperate for a silent place
But scared of a dark room with nothing in
So she's a hurricane a tidal wave
She says
Oh my GOD
That's so FUNNY
I can't believe that, Ha ha HA
Know yourself young ketamine honey
Keep pushing
Gonna push too far

One a.m. now the mind won't tessellate
the mind won't tessellate
Two a.m. now the mind won't tessellate
the mind won't tessellate

Three a.m. now the mind won't tessellate
the mind won't tessellate
Four a.m. now the mind won't tessellate
the mind won't tessellate
Five a.m. now the mind won't tessellate
the mind won't tessellate
Six a.m. now the mind won't tessellate
the mind won't tessellate
Seven a.m. the mind won't tessellate
the mind won't tessellate

There are real seas crashing out that picture
There are megaton waves coming at us
And on the cliffs there's a black figure
Soundless, yelling out great sadness
There are hands in the cracks in the ceiling
Fidgeting scaly and small
They're very lonely, they want me, I feel 'em
Their parents shift and giggle in the wall
The wall's livid, the street paints teeth lights on it
Orange against raw grey
A machine screams down Leaside
and I screw up
And wait for the day...

One a.m. now the mind won't tessellate
the mind won't tessellate
Two a.m. now the mind won't tessellate
the mind won't tessellate
Three a.m. now the mind won't tessellate
the mind won't tessellate

Four a.m. now the mind won't tessellate
the mind won't tessellate
Five a.m. now the mind won't tessellate
the mind won't tessellate
Six a.m. now the mind won't tessellate
the mind won't tessellate
Seven a.m. the mind won't tessellate
the mind won't tessellate

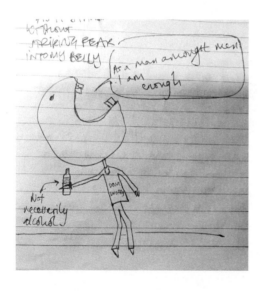

## DAYLIGHT CAME

*Daylight came*
*And drew you naked*
*You you naked*
*On your bed*
*Peace and joy*
*All you lost children*
*Ah you lost children*
*Peace and joy*

# RISING SON

Is everything OK at number 32?
There's an ambulance yelling murder blues
And banging through the nights have you
heard the news? Apparently Rita popped a gasket
She's been hurtling and chortling all over town
Singing weird and loud looking so profound
But they got her in a box and so it's kosher now
Apparently Rita popped a gasket
She wouldn't pay her gas so they cut her off
So she cooked on barbecues in the buff a lot
Swinging boobies to the breeze yelling mazel tov

Poor woman
Rita popped a gasket
Stinking fumes
They complained at number 35
So she moved the barbecues and joyous words inside
Peter says if she continues she'll be burnt alive
Someone should get her shackled up and certified
'It's for her own good' reads the expert advice
She's been quiet all her long lacy curtain life
And now she's looking like an angel in a certain light
Lock her up quick / Rita popped a gasket

*MOVE out this city*
*I'm meant to be the rising sun*
*I'm meant to be the rising sun*
*MOVE out this city*
*I'm meant to be the rising sun*
*I'm meant to be the rising sun*

*Waaaa... the nasty eyes... nuhnuhnuhnuhnuh*

And like a hunchback
Eyes to the asphalt
Pat walks by trying to hide from the catcalls
Spilling from the scaffold
Anywhere she seems to pass
She carries oceans
They only see her teats and arse
For validation
She's heading to the church hall
It's dark there and there's never any curveballs
Soft tunes and the one ray of sunlight
Run baby run say you come for the love of Christ
'Nother lie in the tapestry of subagendas
Lullabies for the blaggers and the moneylenders
Posh kids look daggers at the young offenders
Then spend their inheritance on class A's
And Eddy watches as Clapton becomes expensive
The betting shop
Is the last thing that's unpretentious
So he says as he squanders his mama's rent
It's fuckin endless
Too long since summer's come along to cleanse us
And we're up against it and it is up against us
And if you're not pissed off you are unattentive
I think I read that on a T shirt once
And now I must
Run
That's my bus
That's my bus

*MOVE out this city*
*I'm meant to be the rising son*
*I'm meant to be the rising son*
*MOVE out this city*
*I'm meant to be the rising son*
*I'm meant to be the rising son*

*Waaaa… the nasty eyes… nuhnuhnuhnuhnuh*

*My lover keep your head*
*down hood up run*
*My lover keep your head*
*down hood up run*
*My brother keep your head*
*down hood up run*
*My love keep your head*
*down hood up run*
*My brother keep your head*
*down hood up run*
*My brother keep your head*
*down hood up run*
*My love*
*You could be anyone*
*Anyone…*

Interludes should

→ Reflect the world (collapse of the) through the dream

→ - Reflect the dream (collapse of the mind
thru the world.

# MY MAMA

My mama's in a wheelchair now
But she'll get out and run
My mama raises her eyebrow
High like she raised her son
My mama carries all them bombs
That she was born among
You don't wanna mess with my...

My mama's not an old time nun
Though the time she comes from's hard
My mama's got a quick draw tongue
and a titan size of heart
Ooh, she gives you hot steam food
and a soup of greens she grew
There is love in all the things she do...

And I will come visit you
I will bring fruit and games
I will come anytime you call
I will come visit you
I will bring fruit and games
I will come any time...

My mama is a song of praise
and a daft old nonsense song
My mama swings a vorpal blade
and the jub-jub day's undone

My mama by the Tum Tum tree
with a gorgeous summer's mind
My mama's only five foot two
but she rolls like nine foot nine...

So go on

Take that ladder
Check that ladder
Clip that ladder and climb
Take that ladder
Check that ladder
Clip that ladder and climb
Take that ladder
Check that ladder
Clip that ladder and climb
No mama don't pay that woman no
mind...

My mama's in a wheelchair now
But she'll get out and run
My mama raises her eyebrow
High like she raised her son
My mama carries all them bombs
That she was born among
You don't wanna mess with my...

# FEVER (TIMOTHY IS EVERYWHERE)

Madness and fever.
Things are different now.
I will not be what I was before Thursday.
Men are shouting Go Home to girls born in Burnley.
and monsters are beeping in the trees.
Timothy is everywhere

# I FREAK OUT

I freak out / I get monster mind lean
When I beat out / my head pumps a hype steam
Like an eel out my pipe / tight / the night long
The beasts out there climb on the pylons and
stare / it's not that I'm scared / I'm Terri

fied      I      ride      the      night      sweaty

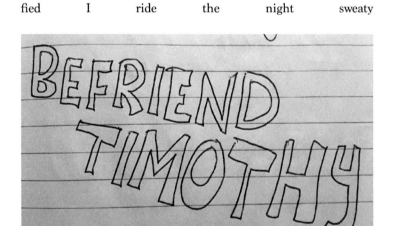

Eyes are wide the mind heavy
Watch the spiders try get me
They get me tangled again
In thrall to all tarantula men
Their lairs is all damp and obscene
Small hairs on 'em
I scramble I scream

I run
I twist I rage
The fist comes hits my face
The girders bricks and blades
Everybody wants me dead
I swear

I freak out in hot rooms
I freak out in hot rooms
I freak out in hot rooms
I freak out in hot rooms
I freak out in hot rooms
I freak out in hot rooms

Everybody's down the pub without me
Everybody's down the pub without me
Everybody's down the pub without me

I freak out I freak out I freak out I freak out  I freak out I freak out / I
freak out I freak out I freak out I freak out I freak out I freak out

Everything's fine... everything's cool... everything's fine... everything's cool

*Two slugs on the catfood*
*Feels like they're on my brain*
*Feels totally insane...*

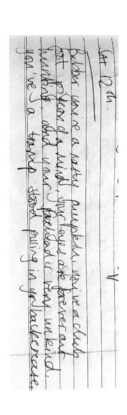

# OI OI

OKAYYYYY!

Oi Oi

Oi Oi

Oi Oi

Can anybody please explain what the fuck is happening?

Can anybody please explain what the fuck is happening?

Can anybody please explain what the fuck is happening?

*Don't claim like you... wait...*

Can anybody please explain what the fuck is happening?
Everybody's stabbing everybody's gone mad again
Yelling in the flats / hear a banshee scream
*You're a bad seed / you're a God-damn bad seed*
I saw
One round-hatted Jew running
Two drunks throwing Nazi salutes chuckling
Three kids jack a phone off a German
And four men at a bus stop ignore them
I saw a crowd with placards in their work clothes
Chanting for tolerance in perturbed tones

I saw a cop with a tit for a hat
Pose for a pic with a chap with a pink tutu
I saw a guy do voodoo with his eyes
On the tube on a woman who was most freaked by him
When he got off, she breathed, sighing bodily
And returned to reading of atrocities
I saw a woman change trains on her own
8 months pregnant and blind
I saw a very big man being dragged
by a very small dog called Clive

Who said

*Can anybody please explain what the fuck*
Oi Oi
*Everybody's stabbing everybody*
Oi Oi

*Can anybody please explain what the fuck*
Oi Oi
*To rebegin without roots, the truth is something to shake off*

*Everybody's stabbing everybody*
Oi oi
*A human in middle of data, the brutal rhythm of day job*

*Ah*
*Babber you're a nasty pumpkin*
*You've a clubfoot pigeon for a mind*
*Your eyes are forever out hunting*
*And your forehead is very unkind*

Can anybody please explain what the fuck is happening
Everybody's stabbing everybody's gone mad again
And Mr Ali got stabbed in his Costcutter
Hot blood a-gushing
As he's clasping his gut lover tell me
Please tell me what's occurred today
Tear a strip of T-shirt make a tourniquet
Anybody do first aid?
Anybody speak Turkish?
Ali fades out girl gets squirmish says
Please explain what it all uh means
Could we all just cool our beans
Could we all just breathe
Nah it's all really happening
Here comes a meat wagon and a ambulance
Everyone starts scattering
It's just me and Mr Ali
Who is asleep
Shake him awake paramedic in green
Take him to a place that he'd much rather be
Take him to the valley where the white stones sing in the heat
And the women can make a man weep
Nah Nah kiddy step aside stop bothering
Nee Nor Nee Nor we're going to Homerton
He'll be fine sonny don't try following
You are just a thread in a spool

Oi Oi
Oi Oi
Oi Oi
Can anybody please explain what the fuck

Oi Oi
To rebegin without roots
The truth is something to shake off
A human in middle of data
The brutal rhythm of dayjob...

AHHHHHHHHH

# DAYLIGHT CAME ii

*Daylight came*
*With all her army*
*Crooked army*
*Sodden land*
*Ah you stones*
*Why so heavy?*
*Ah my mother*
*Let me not be mad*

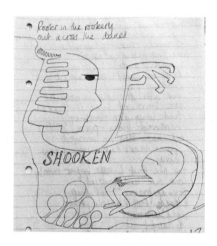

# SHIFT UP FATIH

Here walks the golden panda / to the tinkling of chandeliers
Snaps his fingers and a man appears
Yes sire / speak of your desire to the gushing stream
It'll come in minutes with a white side of double cream
Syllabub / bubble of luxury / rubber bumper bumping rubber bumper subtly
Leagues above the dust and hubbub of the dutty street
Who here keeps the gutters clean?
Where the washing up is done in secret
How long until a conscience
Can become accustomed to the gluttony
Not long sir / Have a salad while you wait
The salmon's coming shortly and I'm sure you're shitting comfortably

*Yes yes daddy history will love you*
*Now shift up Fatih let the people come through*
*You're the excelsior you're the gun you're the dude*
*Now shift up Fatih let the people come through*
*You've got your street names and your statue*
*Now shift up Fatih let the people come through*
*shift up Fatih let the people come through*
*shift up Fatih let the people come...*

Here walks the silver piglet / stumpy legs in
Gilded laminate / scoffing at his troughlet
Pilchard halibut / and ginger peacocks
All in a filo pastry / 'Tis all the freedom
In the field keeps the meat so tasty

'Tis all the women in the basement scrubbing fishguts
Saying piggy gets what piggy wants 'til piggy lifts us
Or tells us the economy has picked up
And gives a fragment of his splendour to the tip cup
Or else until he slips up / and tumbles into normal pain
And walks among us here / where the floors are worn away
'Til then it's polished panels everywhere and winking eyes
and pig defines what is civilised...

*Yes yes daddy history will love you*
*Now shift up Fatih let the people come through*
*You're the excelsior you're the gun you're the dude*
*Now shift up Fatih let the people come through*
*You've got your street names and your statue*
*Now shift up Fatih let the people come through*
*shift up Fatih let the people come through*
*shift up Fatih let the people come...*

You're doing very well at being normal

# CREATURES IN THE CEILING

Creatures in the ceiling
Creatures in the ceiling
Creatures in the ceiling kicking dirt around
Creatures in the ceiling
Creatures in the ceiling
Creatures in the ceiling kicking dirt around
Creatures in the ceiling
Creatures in the ceiling
Creatures in the ceiling kicking dirt around

I'm kipping beneath 'em
In my dirty trousers
Dreaming kingfishers in the dirty south
Flight of small sparrows
Splashing of the oars
Paddle through the mangroves
Salt is in my sores
The crabs are having tantrums
The boatman's very lean
The cargo is some hand drums
And a keg of kerosene
With an inverted cockerel in a box up in the bows
A woman yelling out like there's rocks up in her mouth
Screaming 'bout her babies and the beatings of her mind
The mangrove is pop-suck-squeaking in the tide
And evening's advancing with a peachiness of sky
Pulling colour from a far recess of the eye

The canoe moves through it with a flexing of the arm
Of the boatman and the passengers are pensive and we're calm
All except the woman who is utterly insane
A big red button of a brain
All except the woman and the cockerel in the box
Who screams like as if to wake the monsters of the swamps

Creatures in the ceiling
Creatures in the ceiling
Creatures in the ceiling kicking dirt around
Creatures in the ceiling
Creatures in the ceiling
Creatures in the ceiling kicking dirt around
Creatures in the ceiling
Creatures in the ceiling
Creatures in the ceiling kicking dirt around
Creatures in the ceiling
Creatures in the ceiling
Creatures in the ceiling kicking dirt around

# I THE UNMASTER

I the unmaster / Dream in all colour
Student forever / Plumb the far reaches
Don't stew in errors / Summarise moments
Learn to take notice / I enter openings
I the unmaster / Glimmer in brokeness
Love all your breakage / All of God's infants
Learn every instant / Stream live in ten D
Big heart the bearer / Student forever
I the unmaster / Mind is a spider
Cranked up awareness / Dank little corners
Cramped dutty basements. Bang tidy basslines
Every vibration. Taken in
Mind is a spider. Souped up awareness
Cocktail receptions. Arty proclaimers
Namedropper namers. Pricy snack nibblers
Taken
In

I the unmaster / Taking on water
Colander dreamboat / Paper plane ego
Arctic in speedos / Nut freezer offer
Touch me I shiver / I the unmaster
Turbo shitgiver / Ultra inflater
Molehill to K2 / Mind Himalaya
Silly boy rilly / Least I'm a striver
Strong hearty hugger / I the unmaster
Missing my brother / But life's a stunner
Missing my targets / Well wide of bullseye
But life's a stunner / Ain't life a stunner
I the unmaster / I the unmaster
Pringle tube hitter / Rice jar shaker
Sellotape ripper / Bubblewrap popper
Doublecream taster / Granary squeezer
Broccoli cruncher / chilli sauce eater
Double egg poacher / Plate contemplater
This is my fortune / I the unmaster

go everywhere I'm everywhere in the city
with my H4 and my notebooks, I'm a
journalist and I'm describing the condition
of solitude, of strangeness, of likeness, the
mean while eating at the hive, we
gnaw, we unwrap, step into myself.
I am here being truthful. OK

# EVERYBODY HERE'S GOLDEN

Sleepless
Damp twisted sheets
Angular as a word of a lie
I fling up window and out there is
Open throated engines
and a bird of a sky
Timothy slides into quicksand
Good riddance to his murderer's eyes
A gurgle and he's gone
It's just me and the garden
Screaming as it bursts into light
Who am I to try and drown it out?
In the urban decline I clock
Finsbury Park with its crown of clouds
Beatific smiles on the down and outs
Buzzed from the first hit of the day
I clock
Buff roofers in the altogether

I clock
A bucktoothed lady with a sticky out belly
Preggers belly button like a cherry on the top

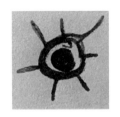

*And everybody here's golden*
*Everybody here's golden*
*Hear the sun stream in*
*Everybody here's golden*
*Everybody here's golden*
*See the sun stream in*

I think of her and I think of her
'Til ambulances are a distant murmur
I turn left towards Rich Mix
Hipster district
I'm switching off my inner judge
I see a man with a gun
in Kevlar, black boots and these dreamy eyes
Like he's thinking of his lover too
Thinking we should have a baby
Thinking
        she's so nice
And people drink tequila do the twist
And I forgive them all for everything
Seeking pleasure for their penises or mouths
Futureless
Trying to shake the sediment
Among the gathering catastrophe
Calm is a super power
I switch mine on

And whatever happens
we are family
and I have reached the venue
and we will be fine hun...

*And everybody here's golden*
*Everybody here's golden*
*See the sun stream in*
*And everybody here's golden*
*Everybody here's golden*
*See the sun stream in*

We could actually do that            Make love
We could actually do that            Skive work
We could actually do that            Have a giggle
We could actually do that            Fall down
We could actually do that            Break our phones
We could actually do that            Snuggle up
We could actually do that            Paint our names
We could actually do that            Run like a nutter
We could actually do that            Look up look up
We could actually do that            Unfriend the Wall
We could actually do that            Get up, walk
We could actually do that            TALK
We could actually do that            TALK
We could actually do that            TALK
why not why not
come on...

# SHOW SOME LOVE

Show some love love / Your
behaviour's strange
For an alien from heaven with
a spaceship brain
Show compassion passion /
Your comportment's odd
For a mega-maxi wolf-winged
immortal god
Show some love love / Your
behaviour's strange

For an alien from heaven with a spaceship brain
And show compassion passion /Your comportment's odd
For a mega-maxi wolf-winged immortal god
So show some love love / Your behaviour's strange
For an alien from heaven with a spaceship brain
Show compassion passion / What you got for proving
Shake the dust sunny
Bust a bloody funky movement...

*I'm a wave I'm a wave my darling*
*I arise I arise I'm done*
*All love to the deep beneath me*
*All love to whoever shall come...*

## 8 weeks to fatherhood

Bristol Temple Meads to London Paddington, 7/9/20
From the Dizraeli Patreon page

Bath Spa is scrolling itself away into woodland, fences, sheep, water, and the colours of everything are rich and wide across the eyeballs. The weird stillness that is an almost-empty train with the air sealed in, with the humans masked off from each other, gives occasional way to a long scritching sound as if a branch is scraping down the carriage roof, or a clatter underneath us like we're rolling suddenly over stones... then a sound like the releasing of air.

I am living these days arranged around an intense calm, a cousin of the feeling on day 3 of a meditation retreat, when each thing comes after the other and the taste of cinnamon or the feeling of cold air becomes a carnival of sensation, and is simultaneously also contained in balance.

My facemask smells of biscuits.

In two months I will be either a DAD or in the pre-math of the birth of my twin sons / suns / airs / heirs / family I haven't yet met but towards whom everything in my life is now leaning - the water bottle at my elbow; the sign on the platform; my mind in some way at all moments of my day.

There is an impact coming, and my body is doing the opposite of bracing for it; the muscles of my face and buttocks and shoulders all loosening. Writing that, I just had an image of a soft, immense wave, a huge wall of compost or soil or unknown substance travelling to meet me.

Last night at Bel's table in the pink light of their neon tube with the rain spotting my left arm and the smoke drifting unrushed to the eggshaped moon, I had a sudden clarity, a sense of the last traces of pretence dropping off my and I said to Bel

"Fuck pretending"

and they put on a track by Burna Boy and laughed

"Yeah fuck pretending".

There seem to be some things that my body knows I won't have time and energy for once the wave comes, and it's shedding them for me. Worry. Self-loathing. Pretending.

(I say this now but you know tomorrow I might be trussed up like a dumbed mummy in poisonous rags, my head a mess of self-hating).

But last night and still this morning, and still this evening after this whole day with the grief and anger of the climate protests with the police breaking up everything before it started, with the sense of everything sliding towards the edge and the world's named leaders accelerating the slide, I am sitting in this hurtling train as myself, cleanly and presently, without pretending, feeling the muscle in my right shoulder flex with the movement of my right hand writing.

Here, at last.

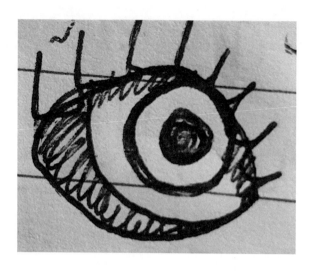

3 weeks to fatherhood

Bristol, 4/10/20

In the absolute stun of the morning, the big clock still going on, the fig leaves spreading wide and clear, the fridge gurgling keenly in his oversize cubbyhole, the taps gleaming as if they'd said something clever. How the devilish fuck is it the Fourth of October?

October promising November promising sons, in the absolute stun of that and Nina now big enough it's hard to believe she can grow more without these babbers bursting out like Jim Carey in The Mask, chaosing the corridors, sudden and immensely strong.

I'm me in my green bomber jacket, me still in my hat and my self-consciousness, me in my fumbling steps forward, and I haven't been given the Dad Key yet, I haven't been shown the secret passage round the side, the lunar ridings, the sump, the grain silos stark and impressive, the wide white sky and the silhouette toiling.

How do I stay myself while all that goes on?

How do I stay in my skin and headbones?

While the maws want milk, the small hands clasp me, the boys fill everything?

Ha. There's a shitness in the culture of parents like the shitness everywhere, that delights in the misery, that loves to say about the sleeplessness and shitfilled pads, that struggles to express the joy.

Come on now, imagine you had the language to express the surging waves, the gathering in of the animals in you.

Imagine you had the forest teeming in your brain and majesty was possible, what then?

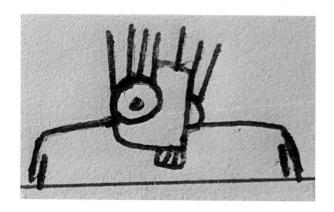

# Beiko Mliba
Tongue Fu ft. Dizraeli & K.O.G. (2020)

By a muddy river / In a murky town
I sit in sirens / Seabirds circling round
I see a gull upon the rooftop without wings
I watch it edging to the edge in mad winds
It's a mirror for within / In a new chapter / In a whipping storm
A cyclone of food wrappers / A kid is born
Nah it's a trace of green
Nah it's a taste of something strange & sweet
It doesn't heal but it makes some peace
Puts a smile on the face of freaks
and it releases from the closet those afraid to breathe
and now we're wading in an army up against the stream
Cos we have seen that there is insufficient day to dream –
One minute Sonny's deep up in the make believe
Next minute Mummy's kneeling at his grave to grieve –

Too cruel / we are cruel and we're angels
We kill life and give life with a movement of the arms
chase dragons in the crucible of Saint Pauls
Topple statues in a revolutionary march
by the muddy river / then we chuck him in
My kids'll not grow up looking up at him
My kids'll not grow up in the ways I did
watching white friends morphing into racist pricks
Never never / the muddy river raising up
I raise a rhythm and a bassline in praise of us
I raise my kids in a toast to the courageous ones
Who kill the devil with a hundred million paper cuts
Singing a change'll come / In the course of all this craziness
I see my mates parade like they were made for this
And they grew up facing shit that I never faced
Still they're turning up the temperature for better days
Still turning up and tracing out the blueprints
for new ways & new architecture / New movements
For new stages / And you could celebrate the dawn
Instead of panicking and sellotaping doors shut
Instead of gazing gormless at the gold framed stories
of the (slave-made) empire that decorate your walls
Look / We celebrate the dawn / We break them ornaments
We work making structures that we never made before
I see my children standing with us at this river
So I'll work until the water comes and elevates us all.

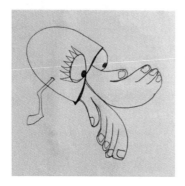

## 2 weeks to fatherhood

aka the Straight White Family

I feel my innards clenching at the threat of the Straight White Family, which is immense in the centre of the landscape of parenting, immense gaudy and gleaming fibreglass clowns & Colgate cheesing : Mum, Dad and the Straight White Kids bursting their fibreglass cheeks with healthy white straightness, I feel them closing in when the lady in the shop beams at Nina & me and approves, when the man in the carpark holds the door for us and approves. Aha, they say, the Straight White Family; all is safe and well.

The depth of approval is profound. I think to moments with male partners; walking past the garage in Brighton; walking past the little girl with her Mummy in Hackney, both of them gaping, my hand in his hand, every cell in my torso screaming alarm circuits, holding hands anyway in spite of; the difference it is for my displays of relationship connection, affection to be swimming in their very own element, a wide warm welcome from the whole of Hollywood, from lovesongs everywhere, billboards bright and wide and tall, the whole world purring and nodding at your love and at the children of it.

I feel gratitude that Nina understands; has lived those same moments in a queer couple, knows better than I do those scowls, that menace.

One of the things that kept me from wanting children in the times I didn't want them was this. And the feeling I had of the sucking vortex with the Straight White Family on the other side, waiting to consume me wholly and stuff my ears with kitchen designs and patios, double glaze my eyes with self-cleaning conservatories & Wagon Wheels.

Let me not be Renault Espaced at the leisure centre with a Diadora mackintosh. Let me not be garden pea'd on the patio by the barbecue staring at the slat fencing. Let me not be locked in a washing machine with a Winnie The Pooh eggcup singing baby magazines.

The Gumtree baby car seat we collected from Keynsham sits in the hall with its ghost baby inside perfectly still, staring.

On the Cykada record sleeve propped by the turntable in the lounge, a boy on the wet sand is silhouetted standing, gaping up at the immense wave curling over him, about to crash down in shimmering fragments. When it crashes, he won't be a boy any more.

# The Kid – EP
(2022)

## THE KID

*still an animal ... still an animal... shake...*
*still an animal*

Conjuring Santa / Conjuring flying saucers
Eyes of a sorcerer / wide portal for fire waters
Magic rain / Reindeer for the sleigh
Imagination / He gave em mysterious names
Poo Bum and Popa Pola / Masher and Boa
Powered by hocus pocus / Kicking the chimneys over
Santa milks em every morning, he fills up a vase
Bangs his elbow / And trickles the milk on his face
Get with the programme yo / It's exceptionally simple
Kid is a wizard / game is conceptual pinball
Anything's thinkable when yr a kiddywinkle
Before God tells us we're sinful / Pre-sex-and-a-pimple
We blaze from the faintest of inklings
Flame takes to the kindling and the fire's lit
He sprays 5D phrases in wingdings
Angels with chromium wings blink at the sight of it

*The kid*
*And here's a honeybomb for anyone who'll listen*
*the renaissance is under four foot tall*
*And he's never heard of money or of fiction*
*The kid is gonna blow your mind*
*Firing honeybombs and wild contradiction*
*The renaissance is popping off the wall*
*He couldn't give a frig for your career moves*
*The kid is gonna blow your mind*
*Blow your mind....*


*still an animal*


My son is an alien
Twin suns in the spaces in his skull
Swims air like a space station
Warps time like a crazy crazy black hole
My boy is a strange one
He's teaching me to become a man
By flinging his banana juice at my shoes
By singing like a red hot vandalous
cantankerous broken amp
Flocks of electric orca
swim through him when he touches water
And as he dries off
His eyes are following the flightpaths of crocodile gods
From where he was before
My son wasn't born in any hospital
He sprang from a fireplace in Tours
In a too-hot winter
Look he's got maps for the end of the world in him

They're coded in the smears in his nappies
Wild deer stampede down the tear tracks on his cheeks
Bruce Lee in a loincloth
My boy's got two teeth in his gums
Two teeth...
And with them he snags beauties by the eyeload
I know no-one like my son
Strange one
Alien

*The kid*
*And here's a honeybomb for anyone who'll listen*
*the renaissance is under four foot tall*
*And he's never heard of money or of fiction*
*The kid is gonna blow your mind*
*Firing honeybombs and wild contradiction*
*The renaissance is popping off the wall*
*He couldn't give a frig for your career moves*
*The kid is gonna blow your mind*
*Blow your mind.... he's gna blow your mind.... blow your mind*

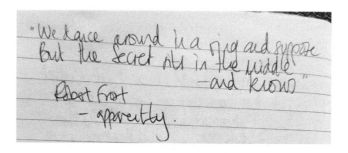

"We dance around in a ring and suppose
But the secret sits in the middle
—and knows"
Robert Frost
— apparently.

1 week to fatherhood

Bristol, 2/11/20

Feels like this should be the start of a new book here with the wind thudding the windows in their frames and N in her sun-coloured cardigan reading a script on her phone, with the calm that is everywhere in us today, it really is although the winds are tearing at the front of the house, Dementors. Now the boys are enormous and sliding whole forearms left to right under N's bellybutton, backs of heads appearing very clearly, I'm sure a small foot was exploring my palm yesterday.

I think we are ready, whatever ready means when you're looking at a shut door this huge, shut fast in its frame with a garden or a galaxy or a corridor on the other side which we can't know but will step into when this door heaves open, which our friends stepped into last night, which our other friends stepped into on Friday, through all the heaving and gore and majesty, the things that happen in the mind in the hours in the hospital, in the muscles around the eyes when you hold your sons for the first time, they are telling me by text that it is wonderful and insane.

And all with these Dementors tearing and thudding the windows, with the world yelling and hauling and hollering, all the world dying outside, falling over and sprouting disasters.

I watch one of the small black flies that've moved in to live with us take off from the folds of my jumper and zigzag up the air in front of me. I look at the faded curtains. N breathes in and out and shifts position. The plants hold perfectly still.

The work this week was finishing the music for a film called We're All Going To Die; watching interviews with men telling me this is the end of all life on Earth, afterwards carrying that familiar strangeness around in my upper belly, the impossible knowledge that this entire planet is becoming hostile to the survival of everyone & thing I love, while at the same time I am radiating love for my two boys turning in the abdomen of a human I love beyond logic... all the details of my life pushed out to a place beyond reason by that impossible knowledge, not making sense at all but making splendour anyway, I mean as if majesty ever had a need for logic, it still doesn't in this moment on a sinking cruise ship with the stars astonishingly vivid and the music bouncing perfect rubber balls around my pleasure vessels, each precious second expanding to the furthest horizon and Nina's skin singing arias at me demanding to be kissed.

I imagine the unreasonable surges of symmetry and protection I might feel for my boys. I imagine this stupid & many-splendoured love chalking a circle around us which no army of puking Trumps could penetrate. I hear talk of severe recession crashing around in the radio.

I know a space that reaches everywhere where there is only calm.

# HOLY HOLY

Are you serious? / I have a mind full of mischief from the science periods
When Mr Malone went bright vermillion trying to teach idiots
Many moons before I hung my shame on my sex and my privilege
Before we became mice-minded men with kiddywinks
Before Nick went / Before time dimmed your brilliance
Back when we huddled round cigarettes like moons
And cassettes passed hands full of punk and Wu Tang Clan tunes
The refrain we'd say was Oi mate

*Oi mate!*

This is Eden / the funfair's in for a day / in for a day
then the council comes to whisk it away
leaving a litter-strewn park and half a stick of candy
floss the kids are randy / Lost they're splitting tabs
and jostling for a lick of mandy
They're off their tits and amped up / somebody stick a ramp up
they're boshing Lynx from out the lid
and Bob's too pissed to stand up
Stacy hold him back / he's starting on older lads
Doing his Hulk impression up and down the cul de sac
Callum's teaching me to roll a fag it's skills for life
lesson five
Lesson six – trying to get inside them polyester tights
I'm in love with Bex tonight / She's wearing a Rugrats T-shirt
the soundtrack is vomit / with poppers for the reverb
What a crock of creatures we were
Seeds of gods and goddesses
Posh kids mixed in with the sons of cleaners

Newly conscious of our penises but not our limits
All of us rocked the Wu Tang / Nobody got the lyrics
Very accomplished mimics though / still in the gleam of after
Birth we learn the shape of words / Fill in the meaning after

*And it is holy holy*
*these are the stones that know me*
*Leave 'em alone and never move them*
*I have built a shrine*
*and it is holy holy*
*These are the roads that growed me*
*I'll take 'em with me to the finish line*
*Finish line*
*All of it holy holy*
*these are the stones that know me*
*Leave 'em alone and never move them*
*I have built a shrine*
*and it is holy holy*
*These are the roads that growed me*
*I'll take 'em with me to the finish line*
*The finish line*

Portrait of the artist as a young eejit
Ornate as a vase sits full of dumb secrets
Always getting arsey with my mum she is
Saintly. Patient. Believing
Giving me love, applauding all my shaky-brained achievements
Making sure that there's a kitchen full of baked potato steam
For me to ride my Raleigh back to every sacred evening
Gravy stained my T-shirt. We called dinner supper
My mama lived through struggle so she aimed for middle upper
We repaid her nicking stuff from Clifton that we could've bought

And Toby taught the ways of mischief to his little brother
Playing knockout ginger. Blims of hash up in the sock draw
Dominic had cable so we watched porn
learning rude German there at number 14,
However small it seems, nothing's deeper than your story

*Cos it is holy holy*
*these are the stones that know me*
*Leave 'em alone and never move them*
*I have built a shrine*
*and it is holy holy*
*These are the roads that growed me*
*I'll take 'em with me to the finish line*
*Finish line*
*And it is holy holy*
*these are the stones that know me*
*Leave 'em alone and never move them*
*I have built a shrine*
*and it is holy holy*
*These are the roads that growed me*
*I'll take em with me to the finish line*
*Finish line*

And if you see him up there tell him Mickey Finn's closed
Tell him I'm still looking in at windows / trying to write raps & meta-
phors / Tell him griptape doesn't scuff my daps anymore
And Stokes Croft is covered in coffee shops like cold sores
Tell him Eddie still never calls up, but it is all love / Tell him kids
smashed the storefront singing my chorus
How d'you like them onions? Tell him I may never break through / but
we'll go for a fuckoff massive skate if I do
It's all holy.

## 6 months of fatherhood

Wazemmes, Lille, France, 12/6/21
9:03am

I can't remember, don't in this instant remember what I dreamed, some shape of it is there with a flat expanse and the consistency of peanut butter, and a human interacting with me... anyway here I am, in the rectangle of park in Wazemmes which has been left to grow into a wild place, fulgurant and beastie, promising lush things, luxuriant shaggy grass-carpet with its daisies and weeds, cigarette butts and secret dogshits all nestled in. In agreement, a Mother tree presides like a tall Dulux dog in a coat of thick thick ivy all the way up to the neckline, deep green, sprouting other species and limitless luxury. I expect pterodactyls to swoop out, and a sloth to be seen dangling.

Six months of fatherhood. Come on then.

The boys are asleep at f***ing last in the pram under the blue cloth with the flowers that used to be our curtain back in the other life. A woman with a pram walks very slowly past, her daughter in braids with pink beads bouncing, and I feel her trust in me; that new trust I've noticed from women with babies who smile knowingly as they walk past : aha, hello sweetness; a man with a pram.

I like it.

Wazemmes. Six months of these Jesus beetles in my days and nights, last night waking in alternate screams, intervals of roughly half an hour, the boys clutching at their ears with inaccurate hands because their jaws are full of pain. Paco now with his two razor-sharp Muskrat gnashers poking whitely through his bottom gums, both he and Idris confused with the pain. It makes Paco fold up like a frog and roll over onto his side; it makes Idris swim on his belly, kicking the hostile air like he could jet off and escape it. These little mofos. These portals, these sunlit explosions, these thieves, these Godlets. If anyone swerves too close to the pram, a wolf leaps up my throat ready to kill.

Two women progress up the park drunkly, very drunkly considering it's 9:15am, with the sloppy swagger of the defiantly drunk. That's right c\*\*ts, I'm drunking cans of F\*\*\* You at 9 of the fifteen A goddamn M in the morning, and all of you can Do One. I watch them go with my wolf eyes narrowed. Danger. Walking through the world with the pram, Papa Wolf is with me constant, watching lorries and dogs and cigarette smoke and crackheads, daring them to slip up and touch my children. Parenthood holds a great violence, sure it's started many wars.

Rainbows, unicorns, cuddlebunnies, violence.

And OK my children, know that I love you in ways so tall it's impossible to write them down, and that I will never in a thousand sleepless nights cause you harm, but when you are screaming bloody murder in my ears for the nineteenth time this hour, and I have not had enough time to breathe or gather calm, and I see the open window and think

I could
just
throw
him
out
and
then
it
would
be
quiet

know that I am human, which is to say a wild animal like you, and that I am in the company of a hundred billion parents before me in that moment, although none of us will say it out loud.

Violence.

Being with babies, like being in proximity with any wild animal, calls out the wild in us too. Wolf, ape, ash tree. And of course not just in violence - as if the world of natural forces were just one of mutual destruction. It calls out the generosity in me, the willingness to give my morning, evening, night to the feeding and protection of these two creatures that look and fart like me. My babies call out a mindlessness, a state of brain in which I am not telling myself stories or rushing down corridors elsewhere, but as present as a container or a blanket; fulfilling a function, simple. This isn't a feeling I've ever had before.

It calls out a stamina too, when I have no more patience at all and I know I have to find some, otherwise what? The window? And I do find patience, and reserves of love off to the sides in pockets I didn't know were there. My back is agony but I can pick up both boys at once and carry them downstairs so that Nina can sleep. Me knees are killing me but I will run three streets back to the van to get the nappy rash cream. My brain is a hot crashed laptop and my eyes are leaden marbles, but I will walk the screaming pram around the streets and construction sites of Wazemmes until the pram doesn't scream, and find a bench among the fag ends of the prehistoric park with its pterodactyls hidden in the ivy, the sloth peeping out, the daisies nodding conspiratorially in the grey air.

A woman in a dayglo trouser-suit slows down as she walks past, and smiles, and I take my yellow notebook and a biro from my bag, exhale, and begin.

# OH MY BABY BOY

Oh my baby boy
Oh my baby boy
We've waited for ya
We've waited for you

Oh my baby boy
Oh my baby boy
We've waited for ya
We've waited for you

And now you're here the rose ain't rotten
and now you're here there's deeper shades
and now you're here the rose ain't rotten
and everything has found its final place

*For Paco and Idris*

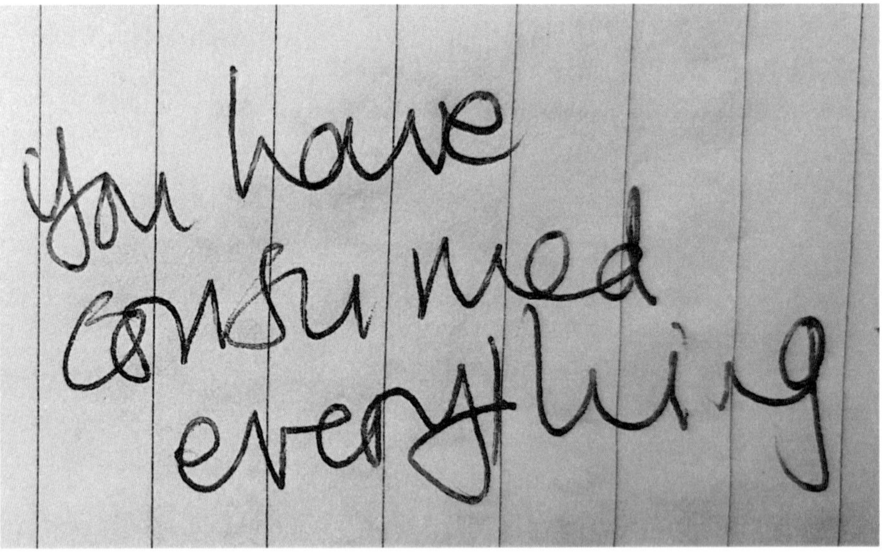
you have
consumed
everything

# Acknowledgements

Thank you Nina. Thank you my Boys. Toby, Mum, Dad. All the humans who've held me and given me courage down the years. You're all everywhere in all of this.

Thank you to my Patreon patrons, you fragrant goslings; you are the consistency that allows the work to happen. I have been able to give this book the time and love I've given it because of you.

Thank you Anthony Anaxagorou for the advice and recommendations.

Thank you Amy Acre for your skilled work at the very last minute pulling it together, pulling me up on spellings and stereotypes, making it look lush.

My community of artists, MCs, wordlovers, noiselovers, aliens, queers, straights and activists who consciously or not, kick me lovingly in the bumhole every day and move me to keep making, pushing, studying. Unmaster.

Thank you Z. Your rejection tipped me into a black hole that I came out of humbler and more present. I needed it.

My fellow travellers at the many stages of the journey : Bad Science, The Small Gods, DownLow, all the others. Love love love.

Thank you Timothy you beady-eyed skank, peering over my shoulder and yanking my ears. You're probably necessary.

Finally and mostly, to everyone who contributed to the 20 Years Deep crowdfunding campaign. You made me promise to make this book of lyrics in exchange for your support. Without that, this would never have got done. I hope that it warms you and helps make sense of things.

Thank you.

# Index of Songs